The ANCIENT BOOKS of IRELAND

ACKNOWLEDGEMENTS

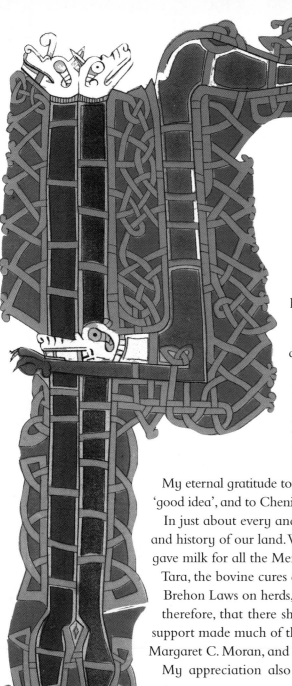

his book is dedicated to all the unnamed scribes and authors who, down the centuries, laboured to preserve Ireland's ancient lore and legends.

My sincere thanks to Aoife, Aideen, Josette and Graham for taking the work to heart and contributing their artisitic talents to make it beautiful.

My appreciation to the keepers of Ireland's books who generously helped in accessing materials for this volume: to Mary Kelleher and Gerard Whelan at the RDS Library, Petra Schnabel at the Royal Irish Academy, Tony Roche of the Department of the Environment, Heritage and Local Government Photography Unit, Sandra McDermott at the National Library of Ireland; to photographers Robert Vance, Tony O'Gorman, Sean Gilmartin, Joe Fanning, Gerry Shanahan and Alain Storme for allowing their pictures to be used.

My eternal gratitude to Dr Pat Wallace and Dr Gerry Lyne for their encouragement, to Katie for saying 'good idea', and to Chenile, Julie and Aoife at Wolfhound/Merlin for their belief in this difficult project.

In just about every ancient manuscript covered in this book there are references to the dairy legends and history of our land. Whether it be the Dun Cow of Cieran, The Tain Bo Cualgne, the Bo Glas that gave milk for all the Men of Erin, the Boroimhe of cattle imposed on the Leinster Men by the King of Tara, the bovine cures attributed to some of our ancient volumes, the honour price of chieftains, the Brehon Laws on herds, the precious vellum for writing material – the cow is central. It is only fitting, therefore, that there should be an association between this book and the Irish Dairy Board. Their support made much of the colour that adorns this volume possible. My thanks to Dr. Noel Cawley, to Margaret C. Moran, and to Pat Ward for their support.

My appreciation also goes to the Heritage Council for accepting this work into its grant aid programme.

Irish Dairy Board

kerrygold

SUPPORTED BY THE HERITAGE COUNCIL

LE CUIDIÚ AN CHOMHAIRLE OIDHREACHTA

This publication has received support from the Heritage Council under the 2005 Publications Grant Scheme.

The
ANCIENT
BOOKS of
IRELAND

MICHAEL SLAVIN

WOLFHOUND PRESS

This First Edition published in 2005 by
WOLFHOUND PRESS
An Imprint of Merlin Publishing
16 Upper Pembroke Street
Dublin 2, Ireland
Tel: +353 1 676 4373
Fax: +353 1 676 4368
publishing@merlin.ie
www.merlinwolfhound.com

Text Copyright © 2005 Michael Slavin
Editing, Design and Layout Copyright © 2005 Merlin Publishing

ISBN 0-86327-928-7

10 9 8 7 6 5 4 3 2 1

Typeset by Carrigboy Typesetting Services
Cover and Layout Design by Graham Thew Design
Cover Illustration by Tom Bulmer
Printed and bound in Portugal by Printer Portuguesa

CONTENTS

THE CELTIC CHURCH

he Celtic Church, out of which these manuscripts were born, had three main periods of development, each of them having a bearing on the literary output produced — 1) the primitive period, 2) the Columban period and 3) the Reform/ Norman period.

1) The most primitive period covers the 130 years that succeeded the arrival of Christianity on this island, up until about AD550, by which time all of the founding fathers had died. Included among them were St Finnian of Clonard (died AD549); St Colum of Terryglass (d. AD549), St Enda of Aran (d. AD530), St Biuthe of Monasterboise (d. AD521), St Brigit of Kildare (d. AD524), St Jarleth of Tuam (d. AD540), St Ciaran of Clonmacnoise (d. AD521).

During this very early period of Christianity in Ireland, only Latin writing was used. Script in the old Gaelic language did not emerge until after the second period of monastic development, which began around AD550. No fragments of this writing survives from earlier than AD600.

Clonmacnoise

Places in ireland most associated with the books treated in this volume.

2) What can be called the Columban Period began and thrived during the active mission of St Columcille from about AD550 to AD597. Among the monasteries he founded were Durrow, Kells and Iona. Contemporary with him were other great monastic innovators like St Brendan of Clonfert (d. AD580), St Comgall of Bangor (d. AD580), St Finnian of Moville (d. c. AD590), St Fintan of Clonenagh (d. AD608), St Kevin of Glendalough (d. AD618). It is to this period that we owe the creation of the *Cathach*, the *Book of Armagh*, the *Book of Kells*, the *Book of Durrow* and many long-lost manuscripts, such as the *Book of Druim Snechta* or the *Book of Monasterboise*, whose existence we know of only through their being mentioned in later works. From the latter part of this time, just prior to the reform of Irish monasticism taking hold in the twelfth century, we also have the *Book of the Dun Cow*, the *Book of Leinster*, the *Annals of Inisfallen* and the *War of the Gaedhil with the Foreigners*.

3) The Reform Period began early in the twelfth-century and was followed by the Norman invasion of 1169. These two movements brought powerful outside influences to bear on the Irish Church and in large part moved the hereditary literary class out of the monasteries into what remained of old Gaelic civilization under the patronage of powerful local chieftains. From this period come the *Book of Ballymote*, the *Great Book of Lecan*, the *Yellow Book of Lecan*, the *Book of Ui Mhaine* and the *Seanchus Mór*, when professional scribes working within localised schools of Gaelic learning continued the tradition of preserving the ancient lore. Later, flowing from that lore, came the *Book of Lismore*, the *Annals of the Four Masters* and *Keating's History of Ireland*.

The beautiful shrine for the *Cathach*.

FOREWORD

I first met Michael Slavin fifteen years ago, and when he invited me to write a short piece to introduce his new venture, *The Ancient Books of Ireland*, I was delighted to accept.

I can describe Michael's new work in the same way as I did his *Book of Tara*, which I launched in 1996, as 'a spot in the middle ground between the world of academia and the purely popular . . .'

Once again Michael Slavin has achieved what he set out to do. With no stinting on research, much of which he carried out at his antiquarian bookshop on Tara, he has written about sixteen of Ireland's ancient books in a familiar and easily accessible manner.

As Director of the Museum of Ireland, I care for Ireland's national material treasures. The National Museum of Ireland's mission is to conserve this magnificent collection while, at the same time, displaying it in the best manner possible for the research, education and enjoyment of people from Ireland and abroad. This book attempts to do something similar for the written word. Extremely valuable and revered literary treasures are put on display for us to study and enjoy. Through technological advances, the pages from these ancient volumes have now become more accessible than ever before. Wolfhound Press has made good use of these techniques in their production of *The Ancient Books of Ireland*.

The author's choice of chronology in dealing with the books is interesting. He decided to treat them more according to the material they contain rather than by the date they were written. He begins in the twelfth century with the Book of the Dun Cow, the oldest volume that tells the ancient pre-Christian legends of Ireland. Later he goes back three centuries to the Book of Armagh, which deals with the arrival of Christianity in Ireland.

Michael admits that the choice of books covered by this volume is based on his own perception of which of our ancient manuscripts have most influenced our perception of ourselves as being Irish. It is an interesting choice, and one that makes for an enjoyable and easily accessible read.

I wish *The Ancient Books of Ireland* every success. It will increase appreciation, both at home and abroad, for the treasures of Irish learning, which have been brought out into the light of day through its well researched beautifully illustrated pages.

Dr Patrick Wallace
Director, The National Museum of Ireland

INTRODUCTION

We Irish like to hold fast to our past. Ancient legends and sagas, stories of heroes, both mythological and real, continue to inform both our picture of that past and the way we view ourselves in the present.

Yet in a strange way, we are more familiar with the content of our legendary past than with the sources from which it is drawn. We know of Cúchulainn and Fionn Mac Cumhaill, of Maeve, Deirdre and Gráinne, but the ancient books from which these tales derive are little known. Great old volumes like the *Book of the Dun Cow*, the *Book of Leinster*, the *Yellow Book of Lecan*, the *Speckled Book of Duniry* or the *Book of Lismore*, which have miraculously survived the rigours of our troubled history, are all but unknown.

Along the way, many volumes have indeed been lost or destroyed, but a unique few have come through to be with us still. Each of these precious heirlooms has its own story and it is those stories that I wish to tell here. They have been fought over, kidnapped, held to ransom, buried, exiled, lost and found again. They were used for cures, venerated as relics and carried as talismans in times of war. In the following ten chapters I try to trace where and how they were written, what happened to them after that, and where they now reside.

Their stories are beautifully intertwined with the history of Ireland. Whether it be in their contents, the time of their writing or the record of their survival down the centuries, they help tell in legend and in fact what has happened on this island of ours from the earliest times. They provide a vital ingredient to our present consciousness of what it means to be Irish and, just as much as the tales they contain, their own stories deserve a telling.

These magnificent old books are not the preserve only of our great libraries or our learned academics, but rather they belong to all of us, and it is in an effort to make that ownership more real that I have attempted this work. In my bookshop here at Tara, I am surrounded by wonderful facsimiles of and commentaries on these ancient volumes. I constantly field questions about them and in the end the passion grew in me to tell their lovely tales. It took a vast amount of reading to put it all together; and that really is all I can take credit for — I have read for you from material that is not easily accessible to the general public and I hope I have done my job well.

I have tried to identify each book through the place and circumstances of its writing, its size, its present condition and the history of its survival. Since the contents of each are vast and sometimes tend to overlap, I have tried only to pinpoint the most important, distinctive and best known material that each of them has brought down to us.

The order in which the books are placed here perhaps needs a bit of explanation, for it is based more on what they contain than on the time they were written. That is why the *Book of the Dun Cow* is treated first, since it is the oldest volume we have that contains the pre-Christian ancient legends. The second oldest in this context is the *Book of Leinster*, followed by the Books of *Ballymote*, *Lecan* and *Lismore*. Then, in chronological order of content, because it has the oldest material on St Patrick, the *Book of Armagh* comes next. Although in itself it is the very oldest book we possess, the Cathach follows on after that in chronology because of its close association with St Columcille.

Studying these ancient literary treasures of Ireland for this book has been a real voyage of discovery for me and a great enjoyment. It has brought me to beautiful places like Clonmacnoise, Donegal, Durrow, Terryglass, Armagh, Kells, Lismore, Duniry, Lackan, Emly and Timoleague to touch the ancient places where they were written. It has also forced me to understand better the history of our land and the people from both here and across the Irish Sea who have tried to lead our people down the centuries. These books have in one way or another come in contact with a myriad of personalities that have helped shape, for good or ill, the destiny of this island. Hence along the way of my study I encountered: Kings of Tara, great churchmen of very differing hues, from St Malachy to St Oliver Plunkett to Archbishop Ussher; political movers like the much-revered Brian Boru to the much-reviled Dermot MacMurrough. The fate of these books at times depended on the actions of people like King James II, Edmund Burke, the warrior bishop Henry Jones or a roving Irish hero like the Chevalier O'Gorman.

I have found the embracing of these great Irish books a most satisfying experience. They are in themselves living legends in which we Irish can take great pride. I hope that my telling of their stories does them justice, for they are part of what we are.

Michael Slavin

HILL OF TARA

Lughnasa, August 2005

Opposite: a page of ancient poems from the *Great Book of Lecan*.

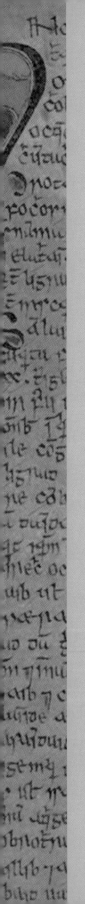

CHAPTER I

Our Oldest Book of Irish Legends

LEBOR NA HUIDRE — BOOK *of the* DUN COW (COMPILED 1090–1106)

N AMED FOR A LEGEND ABOUT ST CIARAN OF CLONMACNOISE, THE BOOK OF THE DUN COW WAS ONCE A SPOIL OF WAR AND HELD FOR RANSOM. WHILE BEING VIGOROUSLY CORRECTED BY ITS EARLY EDITOR, HOLES WERE RUBBED IN ITS VELLUM LEAVES. IT WAS LATER WRENCHED APART AND A RAFT OF ITS PAGES LOST. YET THIS MAGNIFICENT COMPILATION HAS SURVIVED THE RAVAGES OF NINE CENTURIES WELL ENOUGH TO BE HAILED AS:

'THE EARLIEST EXCLUSIVELY GAELIC DOCUMENT THAT WE HAVE;'[1]

'THE OLDEST SURVIVING RECORD OF OLD IRISH LITERATURE;'[2]

'THE MOST ANCIENT SURVIVING COLLECTION OF THE OLD ROMANCES.'[3]

Opposite: Page 99 from the *Book of the Dun Cow.*

BUT ABOVE ALL else the *Book of the Dun Cow* is a window onto Ireland's Celtic past, a transportation into a pre-Christian Otherworld and an introduction to mythical figures like Cúchulainn, Queen Maeve, Emer and Niamh, who remain so much a part of our folklore.

While incomplete in itself through its lost pages, it fills important gaps in other later medieval manuscripts and has been an indispensable source book for early Irish history writers like the Four Masters and Geoffrey Keating. It has been a font of lore for compilers of ancient tales like Lady Gregory, P. W. Joyce and James Stephens, who enthralled new generations with the legends it contains. And it was a well of inspiration for poets like W.B. Yeats, who so beautifully declared that in the stories it contains 'the ancient heart of Ireland still lives'.[4]

The *Book of the Dun Cow* as it is now preserved at the Royal Irish Academy in Dublin.

Heroic legends about Cúchulainn have been illustrated in many books.

It is now generally agreed that this wonderful old book was first copied from earlier, now-lost volumes between 1090 and 1106 at the medieval monastery of Clonmacnoise in County Offaly. This great centre of learning was founded on the banks of the River Shannon in AD548 by St Ciaran (AD516–548), and it is from a legend associated with this reputedly generous and gentle man that *Lebor na hUidre/Book of the Dun Cow* got its unique name. When Ciaran left home for his early studies at Clonard, Co. Meath, a dun cow named Odhar was said to have followed after him and magically provided sustenance for him and his companions. Arising from that story, a legend grew that this book was written on vellum from the hide of Odhar. At this time, ancient books did become objects of veneration. Miracles and assurances of salvation were attributed to them. This is a theme that we will find in relation to many of the volumes discussed here, and we must take these stories in the context of the still very superstitious times in which they arose. Close association with a well-known saint added to the efficacy of a venerated object and thus it was

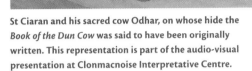

St Ciaran and his sacred cow Odhar, on whose hide the *Book of the Dun Cow* was said to have been originally written. This representation is part of the audio-visual presentation at Clonmacnoise Interpretative Centre.

with *Lebor na hUidre*. Long after Ciaran's death, the skin of Odhar remained at Clonmacnoise as a

Although world famous in its time, nothing is now left of the monastery at Clonard. This fifteenth-century font, from a later church on the site, reminds us of earlier times.

memorial of the founder. It was said that anyone who died while reclined on the skin would go straight to heaven.

Since the legend of Ciaran stated that he used part of this skin to first write down the great epic tale of the Cattle Raid of Cooley (the *Táin Bó Cuailgne*), and because the oldest version of that tale is contained in the *Book of the Dun Cow*, it is not surprising that both the name of the cow and the sacredness associated with her should be passed on to the book itself.

MAEL MUIRE—PRINCIPAL SCRIBE

FROM EVIDENCE written within the book, we know that it had a well-versed cleric named Maol Muire as one its scribes. On page 55 we find the following very practical entry written perhaps at the beginning of a hard day's work, sometime around 1100 in the scriptorium at Clonmacnoise: '*This is a trial of his pen here by Maelmuiri son of the son of Con.*'

We get a bit more information from an inscription written some 300 years later in 1380, on page 37. There we find this note added by the O'Connor kings of Connacht, who at that time were in possession of the volume. '*A prayer for Mael Muire, son of Celechar, grandson of Conn na mBocht [Conn of the Poor], who copied and searched out this book from various books.*'

Mael Muire was indeed the son of Ceileachair (Kelleher), 'a distinguished scholar'[5], and as he stated in his own note on page 55, he was grandson of Conn na mBocht, who in his time founded a hospital for the poor at Clonamacnoise. Conn was also head of the tenth-century fundamentalist religious sect known as *Ceile De* or the Culdees, who were dedicated to the reform of the Irish Church along more ascetic lines (see Chapter 2). Through Conn na mBocht, Mael Muire's lineage could be traced to the anchorite Gorman, who came as a pilgrim to Clonmacnoise and died there in AD610.

All of this brings Mael Muire's intellectual ancestry right back to the time when, according to the best guess of scholars, Irish first became a written language – around AD600. Whatever books of Irish literature were created during the intervening centuries (AD600 to 1100) would have been known to Mael Muire's people. He would also have had access to the oral tradition within the bardic schools, which had kept knowledge of the ancient legends alive, even though many of the books were destroyed in the Viking and Irish wars, when Ireland's places of learning were repeatedly ravaged during the two centuries that preceded Mael Muire's time.

Between AD834 and 1012 Clonmacnoise itself was plundered at least twenty times by either the Vikings or by warring Irish kings like Feidhlimidh of Cashel, who alone raided it on three occasions. But then after the definitive defeat of the Danes by Brian Boru in 1014 and prior to the disruptive arrival of the Normans in 1169, there was a time of relative calm in Ireland's history, which gave a unique window of opportunity for intellectual life to prosper. During the latter part of the eleventh century and into the beginning of the twelfth, the likes of Mael Muire took full advantage of this fragile peace as they committed themselves to saving Ireland's ancient literature from extinction. Hence the *Book of the Dun Cow.*

In this facsimile copy of page 55, the capital T at the top of column one on this page of *Lebor na hUidre* identifies the beginning of the oldest extant version of the great epic story of the Táin. The highlighted text at the top left reads as follows:

*'Táin Bó Cuailgne here below
A great host was assembled by the
Connacians, that is by Aolill and by
Medhbh and messengers went from
them to the three provinces....'*

The now very faint inscription at the top right-hand corner gives an indication of its having been written by the scribe Mael Muire, son of Kelleher, who died during a raid on Clonmacnoise in 1106:

'A trial of pen by Mael Muire...'

MORE THAN ONE SCRIBE

Down through the centuries students of the *Book of the Dun Cow* simply accepted that Mael Muire was its sole author because of the inscriptions on page 55. That is until 1912, when the much-respected handwriting expert and manuscript scholar R.I. Best declared that there were at least three different scribes involved. He identified:

1) a principal writer who was responsible for 80 of the still remaining 134 pages.

2) a contemporary assistant, who wrote 16 pages.

3) a slightly later authoritative contributor who acted as corrector, interpolator and general editor. This person has to be credited with 37 full pages, while in the form of corrections, interpolations and additional notes his handwriting, in one form or another, can be found on a total of 74 pages. In places he so vigorously erased some of the other scribes' work to make room for his own that he rubbed holes in the vellum.[6]

In this new multi-scribe scenario Mael Muire was either the main scribe or the interpolator. Whichever, it does not alter the fact that he was a major contributor and that his involvement enhances the length and depth of the tradition on which the book is based.

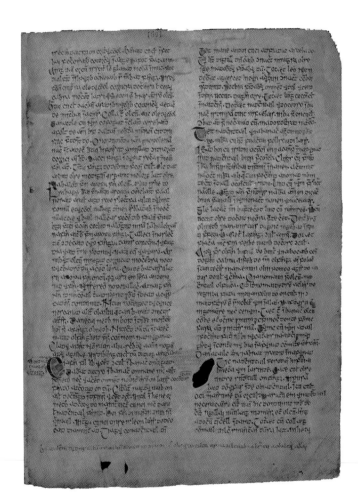

After it had been written, *Lebor na hUidre* was 'edited' by another scribe, and in the process a number of holes were rubbed in its vellum leaves. This one at the bottom of page 69 is in the midst of a story about Queen Maeve.

PRESERVING THE LEGEND OF
THE IRISH PAST

WORK ON *Lebor na hUidre* does appear to have been part of a determined effort at replacing material that had been destroyed during the Viking raids on Clonmacnoise. Having exhausted what remnants were still available to them at their own monastery, one can imagine its scribes setting out from their Shannonside home, with vellum-filled satchels on their backs, in order to undertake what must have been perilous journeys into Meath, Louth and perhaps further north in search of materials preserved in other centres of learning like Monasterboise or Bangor. At Monasterboise they surely sought out now-lost volumes like the book of *Drum Sneachta* (whose origin is thought to have been at a place then known as the Snowy Ridge in Monaghan) or the *Yellow Book of Slane* — both of which are actually mentioned in the text.[7] The material in these early sources has been aptly called 'the product of the heroic age of Irish literature, that time between the seventh and ninth centuries when king and monk and poet co-operated in a passion of memory and creation to build up the legend of the Irish past'.[8]

Preserving that endangered golden lode of lore, during what was to be the last free century of the Gaelic tradition in many parts of the country, is what Mael Muire and his companions were all about and they did their work well in *Lebor na hUidre/Book of the Dun Cow.*

CLONMACNOISE — BIRTHPLACE
OF LEBOR NA HUIDRE

FOR LONGER THAN Oxford, Harvard or the Sorbonne in our time, the great monastic complex of Clonmacnoise was a national and international centre of learning — from its founding by St Ciaran in AD549 at a time when Justinian I ruled the Roman Empire from Constantinople and plague was sweeping across Europe, until its final demise in 1552 when Henry VIII's son, Edward VI, was on the throne of England and Protestantism was on the rise. During that amazing thousand years, students from Ireland, Britain and the Continent came to this Shannonside centre and availed of its superb scholasticism, not only in the religious arts but in a wider range of subjects as well. World scholars like Alcuin and the great geographer Dicuil, both from the court of Charlemagne, studied here in the late eighth and early ninth century. 'From Clonmacnoise in the heart of Ireland subtle waves of influence radiated on her shores and sometimes even beyond her seas,' says antiquarian R.A.S Macalister.[9]

The Irish name *Cluain Maccu Nois* means 'The meadow of the sons of Nos', referring to a family of overlords in this area of County Offaly — the Barony of Garrycastle, seven miles south of Athlone.

The founder of Clonmacnoise, St Ciaran, was born the son of a well-to-do chariot-maker in AD515. Having had his early education with St Finian in the greatest school of the time at Clonard (where St Columcille was a fellow student), he then advanced his spiritual life at the strict monastery of St Enda on the Aran Islands.

While still just in his thirties, Ciaran established a hermitage on Hare Island on Lough Ree. There he attracted a very large following of young monks and they in turn encouraged him to found a religious house and school on the mainland. Through the generosity of a prince of the O'Neill's, Dermot Mac Cerbaill, he was given a meadow by the Shannon which contained a holy well. There Dermot helped him erect the monastery's first wooden post.

The strange story is related that during the ceremony Ciaran foretold that Dermot would soon become high king. The prince's followers immediately set out to make this prophecy reality by slaying the then reigning Tuathal Maolgharbh. Dermot did in fact become king and, like other kings after him, he was a lifelong benefactor of the new monastery.

A depiction on the base of a cross at Clonmacnoise of the beginning of construction at the monastery in AD549, when King Dermot of Tara was said to have helped St Ciaran put the first post in position.

According to the *Book of Lismore* (see Chapter 4), Ciaran survived but a few months after the foundation of Clonmacnoise. He died at the very young age of 33 in AD548. However, so powerful was his personality and so strong was his influence with both royal and religious leaders of the time that his school thrived after him.

In contrast to other scholastic centres such as Bangor or Armagh, which concentrated on Latin learning, Clonmacnoise was for the first 600 years of its existence marked as the headquarters of Gaelic learning. From the twelfth century onwards, Norman influence and the Romanisation of the Irish Church drastically changed that ethos. The Celtic-oriented rule of Columcille was replaced by the Benedictine code imposed by Rome, and it became a more strictly controlled religious school. In this new situation there was no longer room for the traditional hereditary Gaelic scholars. They had to move out and seek support wherever they could among the remaining Gaelic chieftains.

Many books written at Clonmacnoise are now lost, including perhaps an earlier version of the *Book of the Dun Cow*. Surviving along with *Lebor na hUidre* are the much respected *Annals of Tigernach* and the *Annals of Clonmacnoise,* which came from here as well. Both of these books give notations of annual events in world and

Down the centuries Clonamcnoise's ancient landscape has been the subject of many prints and paintings. This one from the eighteenth century by Grose shows one ancient cross in a precarious state.

Irish history from the earliest times down to the early fifteenth century.

Richly endowed by kings of the O'Neill clan and the O'Connors of Connacht, and even by Charlemagne himself, who bestowed 'fifty sicles of silver', Clonmacnoise became a veritable treasury of precious artefacts, and it is no wonder that it was the target of repeated raids and plundering — first by warring Irish chieftains, then by the Vikings and then by the Normans. At least 50 attacks on the monastery and the town surrounding it are recorded in the *Annals*. But such was its strength and depth that it always recovered to carry on the work of learning. However, during the bitter religious wars of Tudor times its final demise came in 1552 when it was razed by the powerful English garrison from Athlone. However, its memory as a sacred place and as a centre of quality learning for over 1000 years lives on. Part of that legacy is the beautiful *Book of the Dun Cow*.

Bishop Healy, in his 1896 book *Ireland's Ancient Schools and Scholars*, is almost poetic in his description of Clonmacnoise: 'How solitary now she sits by the great river that once thronged city! Her gates are broken and her streets are silent. Yet in olden times she was a queen and the children of many lands came to do her homage.'

DESCRIPTION OF THE BOOK

AS IT NOW EXISTS in very safe keeping at the Royal Irish Academy on Dawson Street, Dublin, the *Book of the Dun Cow* consists of 67 vellum leaves, most of which measure 11 inches by 8 inches. Each page has two columns and about 500 words. The renowned book expert Eugene O'Curry estimated in 1861 that it would have taken 500 pages of the *Annals of the Four Masters* to contain even what is now left of the book.[10]

Because of the incomplete state of the volume, no English version of its entire text has ever been published. It is looked upon as a source book rather than a complete narration. All of its contents have, down the years, appeared in various journals like *Celtica* or *Eriu*.[11] If the whole book were published, it would contain 100,000 words and, with translation, would fill close on 300 pages of a printed volume like this one.

Even in its present incomplete form, the *Book of the Dun Cow* still provides a vast amount of material, from which the majority of our best-known ancient Irish tales are born — literature that has helped form our ideas of what it means to be of Ireland.

It is a workmanlike book that has little in terms of decoration. However, at the start of major sections it does have delicate ornate capitals that are tastefully coloured in yellow, purple and red. An older pagination on the back of each leaf dating from before the sixteenth century gives a good indication of just how much of it is now missing. It is thought that at least 66 pages are lost — 51 of them prior to the seventeenth century and 16 more after that. In 1870 Joseph O'Longan created a new pagination for the facsimile he was making for the Royal Irish Academy. This concentrates on only the existing leaves and runs consecutively from page 1 through to 134 and it is this pagination to which I refer here.

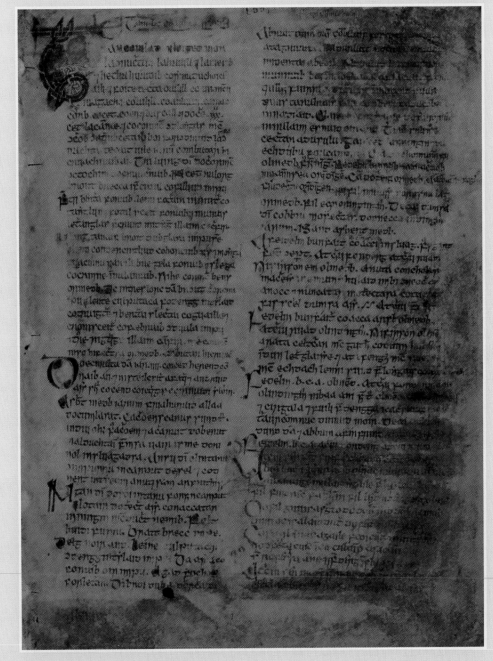

The original text for the beginning of the Táin.

Aerial view of the Clonmacnoise site on the banks of the River Shannon.

CONTENTS OF THE BOOK

SO JUST WHAT IS in the *Book of the Dun Cow* that makes it is one of Ireland's most precious literary possessions? Today, in any of our bookshops, we will find well-stocked shelves of paperback volumes on the ancient tales and sagas of Ireland. As stated earlier, the oldest source we have for that unique legacy from our Celtic past is the *Book of the Dun Cow*. It was compiled to be a 'library' of the most important literature then existent at the end of the eleventh century. What remains of that material is laid out under some 37 headings and falls into the following main categories: Irish Sagas, Historical and Spiritual Tracts, Otherworld Fantasies, Legends of Irish Kings. I will not attempt to list all of the material and will concentrate on the best known items.

THE SAGAS

AMONG WHAT ARE termed 'cattle raid sagas' the most important, of course, is the book's inclusion of the earliest existing version of the celebrated ancient Irish epic the *Táin Bó Cuailgne* (The Cattle Raid of Cooley). Later, more complete versions of this saga are found in the *Book of Leinster* and the *Yellow Book of Lecan*. Here, with some of its folios among the missing, this famous tale still takes up 28 pages at the centre of the book (pp. 55–83).

THE TÁIN

THIS STORY OF GREED, heroism and tragedy derives from oral material that goes back thousands of years to Ireland's pre-Christian past. It reflects a time when cattle were the currency of exchange and also the object of frequent raids by one king or queen into the territory of another. The *Táin* and other related tales contain details of dress, weapons, customs, etc., which indicate that they originated as royal court entertainment anywhere between 400 BC and AD100. The form in which the tale is found here probably took shape in the first century of our era.[12] It was then transmitted orally until it first took

**Queen Maeve
preparing to do battle
with the Ulstermen as
depicted in Mary A.
Hutton's** *The Táin.*

written life sometime during the seventh century in now-lost books. It tells the tale of Queen Maeve's desire to have the best bull in Ireland, which would make her possessions more valuable than those of her husband, King Ailill of Connacht. In order to get this prize she had to go to war with Ulster. Standing between her and victory was the warrior Cúchulainn, 'The Hound of Ulster'. In true heroic style the issue came down to hand-to-hand combat between Cúchulainn and Maeve's champion, Ferdia. These two protagonists were in fact soul friends of long standing and they poignantly bound each other's wounds at the close of each day's combat.[13] Around these themes is built an epic tale of major proportions, which is the most ancient and best of its kind in all of Europe.

Other sagas included are:

'The Cattle Spoil of Dartoid' — just a section of a tale about a plunder of cattle in Munster.

'The Cattle Spoil of Flidais' — this is closely related to the *Táin* and is the story of another raid by the men of Connacht in which they sought supplies for Queen Maeve's army camp.

'The Intoxication of the Ulstermen' — the story of a frenzied raid from the north deep into Munster.

'The Cause of the Battle of Cnucha' — this introduces us to Cumhaill, the father of Fionn Mac Cumhaill, hero of the Fianna Cycle of tales which are centred on the monarchy of Tara and Cormac Mac Airt.

'The Feast of Bricriu' — the tale of trouble-maker Bricriu, who deliberately sets the heroes of Ireland at each other's throats over the 'Champion's Portion'.

Also spread through the book are other stories relating to Cúchulainn — his conception, his courtship of Emer, his contacts with the Otherworld in 'The Sick Bed of Cúchulainn' and 'The Phantom Chariot of Cúchulainn'.

HISTORICAL AND SPIRITUAL TRACTS

'SIX AGES OF THE WORLD' — As with many other medieval Irish manuscripts, the book begins with a historical tract on the 'Invasion Legends of Ireland' (the *Lebor Gabála Érenn*), which purports to tell of pre-historic times in Ireland and the successive arrival here of peoples like the Parthalonians, the Fir Bolg, the Tuatha De Danann and the Milesians. This is the earliest written reference we have of this long tract. There were previous versions but they no longer exist. Sadly, here in *Lebor na hUidre*, because of its lost pages, we have only a fragment of the tract remaining (but it does appear that they were present when the Four Masters were working on their version of the *Lebor Gabála Érenn* in 1631 (see Chapter 10)).

'The Story of Tuan' — This is an Otherworldly vision in which the spirit figure Tuan takes on animal and bird shapes as he observes the soul of Ireland evolve during the various incursions onto the land of Erin by the Parthalonians, the Fir Bolg and the Tuatha De Danann, from the earliest times until the coming of the Gaels. This theme is expanded upon in the versions of the *Lebor Gabála Erenn* found in the *Book of Leinster, Book of Ballymote, Book of Lecan*, etc.

'The Nennius History of Britain' — just a fragment of an Irish version of Nennius's *Historia Brittonum*, which in this segment has to do with St Ambrose's confrontation with the Druids of Britain. There is also a small section on St Patrick.

While the book's main focus was to preserve the ancient pre-Christian lore, the scribes were religious men working within a monastery environment, and thus it is no wonder that material of a pious nature was interspersed. Among the tracts included are:

'Tidings of Doomsday' — a three-page discussion of the Day of Judgement.

'Two Sorrows of the Kingdom of Heaven' — another discussion of the Last Day and the conflicts of Enoch and Elias with the Anti-Christ.

'Tidings of the Resurrection' — a long three-page sermon on the Resurrection.

'Eulogy of Columcille' — Although incomplete here, this poem in praise of the great Columcille still runs for over ten pages and is second only to the *Táin* in length. It was first composed by a leader of the *filí* or aristocratic poet class, Dallan Forgail, soon after Columcille's death in AD592, and is an encomium of this powerful church leader, who at the important convention of civic and church leaders at Druim Ceit in AD575 acted as mediator for the poets in their dispute with the kings of Ireland and Scotland — thus saving their livelihoods. On page 15 there is a hymn that is attributed to Columcille himself.

OTHERWORLD FANTASIES

The book preserves the most delightful selection of fantasies, in which the cast of characters flit between human reality and the Otherworld — a place of the spirit which for all time will be one of refuge for the volatile Irish psyche. W.B. Yeats beautifully enunciated this in his soul-rending poem 'The Stolen Child':

'Come away, O human child!
To the waters and the wild
With a faery, hand in hand,
For the world's more full of weeping than you can understand.'[14]

Here is a selection of these crossings over between this world and the Otherworld, as found in *Lebor na hUidre*:

'The Courtship of Étaín' — one of the most abiding of Irish love tales, in which Étaín first knew the love god Midir, was then transformed into a butterfly, returned to human form, married the king Eochaid Heremon of Tara but was then spirited away once more by Midir.

One of the magnificent love stories recorded in the *Book of the Dun Cow* is that of Étaín and Midir's escape from Tara when turned into swans joined by a golden chain. This depiction of that tale by artist Desmond Kinney adorns the foyer of the Irish Dairy Board offices in Dublin.

HISTORY OF
LEBOR NA HUIDRE

1106

Lebor na hUidre must have been completed before 1106, as this is the date that Mael Muire met a violent death. Under that date the *Annals of the Four Masters* state: 'Mael Muire, son of Mac Cuinn-na-mBocht, was killed in the middle of the Daimhliag of Cluain-Mic-Nois by plunderers.'[15]

1178

The Norman settlement of Ireland began in 1169 and over the next ten years, as the newcomers extended their control right across the midlands, Clonmacnoise's situation became more and more precarious. When De Burgo raided the monastery in 1179, 105 houses were burned. It is a safe assumption that the revision of the *Book of the Dun Cow* by 'the Interpolator' had been completed prior to that date. And also before that time the book, along with other sacred objects like its companion volume *An Lebor Gearr* (*The Short Book*, now lost), must then have been taken away to safety by either the O'Connor kings of Connacht or the O'Donnells of Donegal, who, in the tradition of their kinsman Columcille, had down the centuries demonstrated a supreme respect for books. Over the next 200 years the *Book of the Dun Cow* and *An Lebor Gearr* were to change hands a number of times between the royal houses of Connacht and Tir Conaill.

1380

The book itself takes up its own story at this point. According to a note written into a blank space on page 37, we know that during the reign of Conchobar, son of Aed, who was king of the O'Donnells between 1356 and 1380, *Lebor na hUidre* was given by him in ransom for a young boy of his people, who had been taken hostage by the O'Connors of Sligo. Referring to the book and its companion, it reads: ' ... *and in the time of Conchobar son of Aed O'Donnell they were taken to the west, and in this manner they were taken — the Leabar Gearr in* ransom for O'Doherty and Leabar na Huidre going in ransom for the son of O'Donnell's olav of history, it being taken by Cathal as a pledge for him from Cenel Conail [the O'Donnells].'

A further note on page 37 indicates that in 1380 the O'Connors ordered the re-inking and restoration of faded pages by the poet Sigraid O'Cuirrndin, who died in 1388. The *Book of the Dun Cow* then remained under the protection of the kings of Connacht for the next 82 years, until it was won back in battle by Red Hugh O'Donnell.

— 1470 —

After its triumphant return to Donegal, confirmation of the recovery of the book by the O'Donnells was thus recorded on page 37: '*A prayer for Aed Ruad son of Niall Garb O'Donnell who carried off this book by force from the Connachtmen and the Leabar Gearr along with it after it had been absent from us from the time of Cahal Og O'Connor to that of Ruaidri son of Brian O'Connor.*

The *Annals of the Four Masters* dates this event at 1470 and notes: 'The Castle of Sligo, held by Domhnall son of Eoghan O'Connor, was taken by O'Donnell after he had besieged it for a long time, and O'Donnell dictated his own terms, including submission and tribute from lower Connacht. It was by these terms that the *Leabar Gearr* and *Leabar na hUidhre* were given to him, which had been taken to the west in the time of Sean O'Connor . . . '[16]

The highlighted notes on page 37 tell the book's authorship and its story between 1380 and 1470 when its ownership was the subject of bitter conflict between the O'Connors of Connacht and the O'Donnells of Donegal:

'Pray for Moelmuiri, the son of Ceilechar, that is the son of Con na mBocht, who wrote and collected this book from many books. . . .'

Also:

'A prayer here for Aedh Ruadh son of Niall Garbh O'Donnell, who forcibly recovered this book from the people of Connacht. . . .'

—— 1630 ——

The next we hear of the book is 150 years later in AD1630 when it was still in Donegal and being used as a reference by the authors of the *Annals of the Four Masters*. The O'Clerys refer to the book in their *Martyrology of Donegal* (1630) and appear to have had it at Donegal during work on the *Annals* and for their *Lebor Gabála* (1631). At this period of Irish history writing, the book was also referred to by historians John Colgan in his *Acta Sanctorum* (1645) and Geoffrey Keating in his *Foras Feasa ar Éirinn* (1632–6).[17]

—— 1839 ——

The book then disappears from history once more for another 200 years and re-emerges only in the 1830s when it is quoted by the great nineteenth-century antiquarian George Petrie in his celebrated book *History and Antiquities of Tara Hill*. He notes that he examined the book and found it to be in 'mutilated form'.[18] He also says that it was then in the possession of Dublin book publishers Hodges and Smith. How it came into the hands of this College Green firm we have no way of knowing, but in 1844 they sold the book along with 212 other manuscript items to the Royal Irish Academy for the then bargain price of 1200 guineas. It has remained with the Academy ever since.

—— 1870 ——

Due to the many requests received by the Royal Irish Academy from scholars wishing to view the book, in 1870 they commissioned Joseph O'Longan to create an exact lithographic facsimile. This superb penman, the best of his time, laboured under the difficulty of not knowing that he was dealing with three different sets of handwriting in the 134 pages of script. A limited edition of 200 copies were printed and while some scholars were critical of the effort, it did make the old book available to a wider readership than ever before. The Academy had the original re-bound in 1881 and sadly this was a disaster, which had to be corrected later on. In the manner of Victorian bookbinding, each of the 67 leaves were separated from that adjoining it, thus making it impossible for scholars to determine the true order of the pages.

—— 1912 ——

It was not until 1912 that handwriting expert R.I. Best made the discovery that three hands were involved in writing the book. Following on from this study, Best and fellow expert Osborn Bergin were commissioned by the Royal Irish Academy to complete a new definitive Irish edition in which the sections attributed to the three scribes are distinguished by three different fonts of Roman type. This copy was published in 1929.[19]

—— 1967 ——

The Academy set about correcting the bindery mistakes of 1881 by asking Robert Powell to take the book asunder once more and re-bind it. During this painstaking process, which used the most sophisticated technology of the time, he and his team were able, with a good degree of certainty, to once again pair 44 of the 67 leaves with their original conjugates. Some questions still remain regarding the proper order of the other 23 leaves.

—— 2002 ——

At the beginning of the new millennium the latest technology has again been applied to the *Book of the Dun Cow* and now all of its 134 pages have been digitally scanned and entered on the World Wide Web. After almost 900 years of its existence, this grand old volume is now available to billions all over the world on the ISOS website at www. isos.dcu.ie, which is a co-operative effort between the Royal Irish Academy and Dublin City University.

This then is the story of Ireland's oldest book of ancient lore — one that has had a huge influence on the later writing about our legends, history and early social customs. While having a marked impact on how we Irish view our past, *Lebor na hUidre* has itself remained relatively discreet and unknown. I hope the above goes some way toward changing that for you the reader.

CHAPTER II

The Great Pre-Norman Codex
BOOK *of* LEINSTER *or* LEBOR NA NUACHONGBALA
(1152–1161)

WRITTEN ON THE SHORES OF LOUGH DERG AT TERRYGLASS, TIPPERARY, JUST PRIOR TO THE ARRIVAL OF THE NORMANS, THE BOOK THEN SPENT THE NEXT 400 YEARS IN THE CARE OF THE O'MOORES NEAR THE ROCK OF DUNAMASE IN COUNTY LAOIS AT OUGHAVAIL. FROM THIS PLACE IT TOOK ITS ALL BUT UNPRONOUNCEABLE NAME LEBOR NA NUACHONGBALA (NOOA – CONG – WALLA). DURING THE TROUBLED SEVENTEENTH CENTURY ITS IDENTITY WAS LOST, AND DOWN THE YEARS IT HAS BOURNE VARIOUS TITLES – LIKE SHELF NUMBER 122.229, THE BOOK OF GLENDALOUGH AND NOW THE BOOK OF LEINSTER.

**Opposite: Invasion Legend
page from the *Book of Leinster***

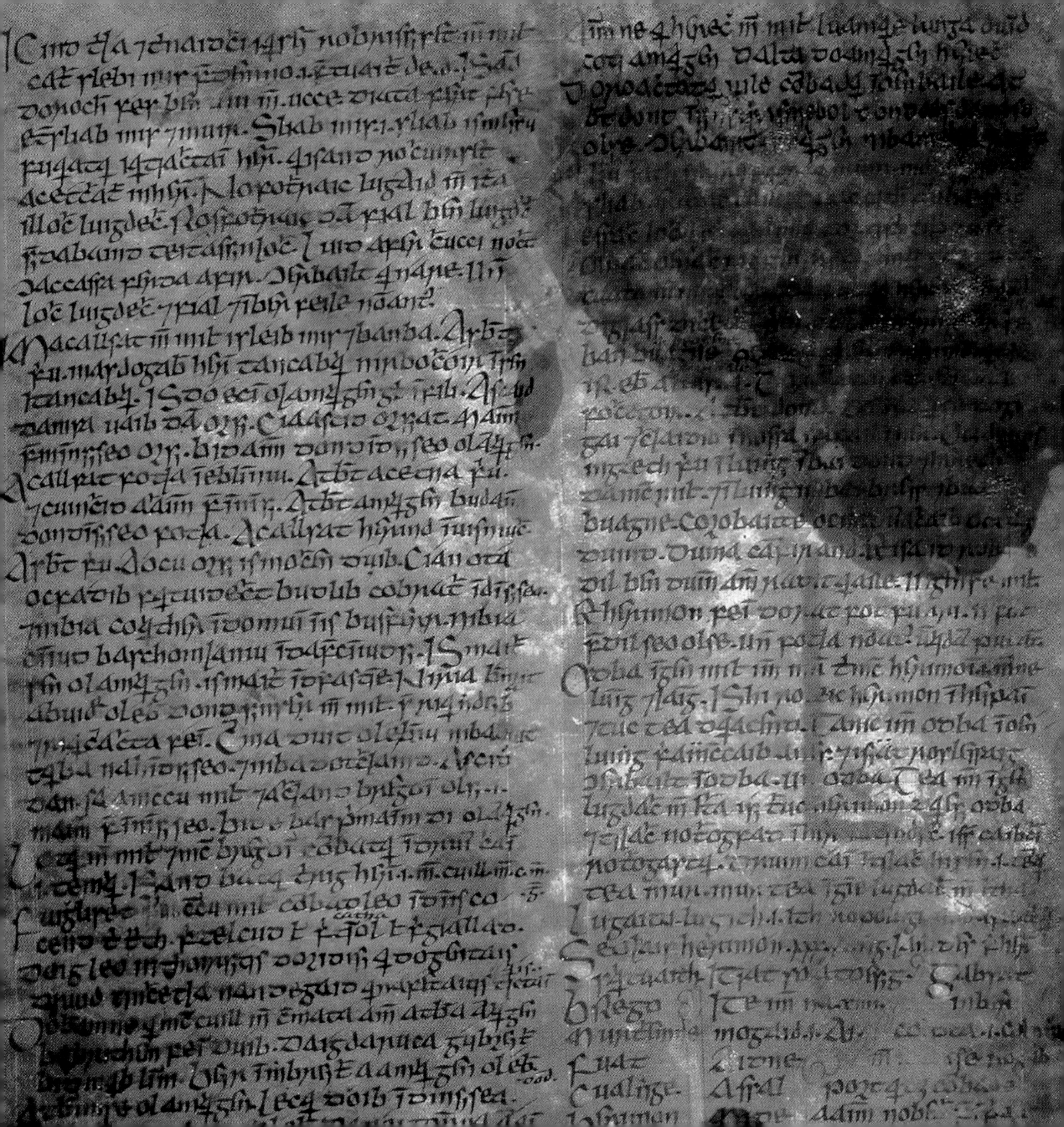

his is a bulky compendium of 187 tall vellum sheets, generally measuring about 13 inches by 9 inches. According to Eugene O'Curry, the words crammed onto the front and back of its folia would fill 2000 pages in the *Annals of the Four Masters* — four times his estimate for the *Book of the Dun Cow*.

Just as with the *Dun Cow*, this compilation of ancient lore, made in the mid-twelfth century, was intended as a library of then available material, but it goes far beyond its predecessor not only in size but in the scope of subject matter it covers.

Images of Irish kings from Knockmoy Abbey in Galway.

It is a *sacred* book in that it introduces us to the Otherworld panoply of gods in pre-Christian Ireland. Its all but complete version of the *Lebor Gabála Erenn* or the Book of Invasions is at the heart of what is called the Mythological Cycle.

It is a *royal* book because here for the first time we find the Roll of Irish Kings. This is a listing and brief description of what were called the high kings of Ireland. Lists of more local kings were also given. The book also includes detailed and fabulous descriptions of regal festivals at Ireland's ancient royal seat on the Hill of Tara.

It is a *warrior* book because of its long version of the *Táin Bó Cuailgne* and its inclusion of a substantial amount of material on Fionn Mac Cumhaill and his Fianna.

It is a *historical* book because of notes added during the course of its eventful lifetime that enlighten us about events in centuries long after its initial compilation, which began around 1152.

Although it has some fascinating pages that include drawings and lightly decorated initial letters, this is basically a workmanlike book in which as many words as possible are crammed onto its 374 pages. For the most part they are in two columns, but on some they extend to three.

The *Book of Leinster* is not its proper title at all. Fourteenth- and fifteenth-century manuscripts identified it as *Lebor na Nuachongbala* — in reference to the townland of Oughavail near Stradbally in County Laois where it was in safe-keeping until the late 1500s, when it was moved to Kildare. There it remained until 1700.

After that it was taken to Britain and for the next 150 years it was simply referred to as 122.229 MS while in the Hertfordshire library of Sir Thomas Sebright, or H.2.18 when in 1782 it came home to Trinity College.[1] Fifty years later Irish antiquarian George Petrie was referring to it as the then-lost *Book of Glendalough*. In 1845, Eugene O'Curry mistakenly thought it was another lost

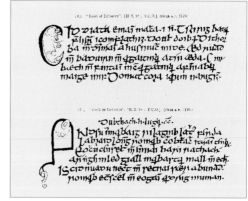

Letters from the *Book of Leinster*.
Although a very workmanlike book, which had as many words as possible crammed on each page, the scribes still found space for some very distinctive letters, like this C at the beginning of a section describing the origin of the sacred site of Emain Macha, or an A at the beginning of a poem stating *'how difficult it is to deal with Leinstermen'*.

document called the *Book of Leinster*. Because of his eminent authority, this name stuck and for the last 150 years it has been known under that name.[2]

Only in 1937 did academics re-discover that it was in fact none other than *Lebor na Nuachongbala*. But by that time it was too late to drop its erroneous title. So, for the present at least, it is officially known as the *Book of Leinster*, formerly *Lebor na Nuachongbala*.

Out of its total number of leaves, 177 of them now reside in their own specially constructed box at Trinity College Library, and although generally known as the *Book of Leinster* they still go by their original shelf number there — H.2.18. Another ten leaves that got separated from the main body back in the seventeenth century are housed in the Franciscan Convent in Killiney, Co. Dublin. Neither section is on general view to the public.

Judging from two foliations that were done when it resided in Oughavail, Co. Laois, at least a further 45 pages have been lost. As a result of constant reference use, the front and back leaves are very worn.

Through a co-operative effort by Trinity College, the Franciscan Convent and Dublin City University, all 187 pages can now be viewed on the World Wide Web at www.isos.dcu.ie.

During a lecture on what he had named the *Book of Leinster* back in 1861, Eugene O'Curry said of this great book: 'I think I may say with sorrow, that there is not in all Europe any nation but this of ours that would not long since have made a national literary fortune out of such a volume, had they been fortunate enough to possess such an heirloom of history.'[3]

THE SCRIBES

Scribes went out from Terryglass to copy material from now-lost books at places like Bangor, Co. Down, and Monasterboice in Louth.

IN RED INK ON folio 32 it says: '*Aed son of Crimthainn wrote this book from many other books.*' As hereditary descendant of the Terryglass monastery's sixth-century founder, St Colum, Aed was *coarb* of the monastery (which lay on the east shore of Lough Derg in County Tipperary), a position that placed him even above the abbot in importance. Until quite recently, on the evidence of this inscription and the basic similarity of all the writing throughout the manuscript, scholars were convinced that the *Book of Leinster* was the work of this one scribe. Whatever differences they did detect were ascribed to changes either of mood on Aed's part, the weather, or the situation in which he wrote.

It was not until 1966 that handwriting expert William O'Sullivan distinguished at least five separate hands in the main composition of the book. He also confirmed that it had been written in several sections that were thonged together at a later date.[4]

Monasterboice, County Louth.

However, Aed Mac Crimthainn still emerges as the chief scribe, responsible for by far the greatest part of the script. His hand is described by O'Sullivan as one of 'character and strength'. Another scribe, said to have 'a fine calligraphic hand', could have been Bishop Find of Kildare, who probably commissioned this work in the first place. Because of distinctive ways of writing certain letters, another two scribes are simply called 'S' and 'U'. One more hand is identified by the letter 'T', since part of his work was on the book's version of the *Táin*. His is a hurried, untidy script, but this does not take away from the important function he filled throughout the book. He appears to have been a type of editor whose insertions tied parts of the contents together and clarified other sections. In addition to his part of the *Táin*, he also contributed an Irish version of the 'Siege of Troy', a number of genealogies and, more importantly, he edited together the 'Lore of Sacred Places' (*Dindshenchas*), which is dispersed throughout the volume.

All of this points towards a huge co-operative effort at bringing together material that was in danger of being lost forever. Once again we can imagine these scribes heading out from the main centre at Terryglass in search of both oral and written material. Just what they were seeking out is indicated within the text itself on folio 151 — the massive number of stories that the ancient *filí* had to know: '*Of the qualification of the poet in stories and deeds, here follows to be related to kings and chiefs: Seven times fifty stories — five times fifty prime stories, and twice fifty secondary stories — and these are the Prime Stories: Destructions and Preyings, and Courtships and Battles and Caves and Navigations and Tragedies and Expeditions and Conflagrations.*'

The book then goes on to name 187 of the prime stories — a list that is thought to have been first compiled around the seventh century. However, many of the stories within it were first conceived hundreds of years prior to that. Only a fraction of these tales are fully narrated in the *Book of Leinster*. So the quest undertaken by the Terryglass scribes must have been a difficult and sometimes frustrating one.[5]

Like an entry to a long-lost past, this old doorway is part of a wall at the ancient monastery site of Terryglass, where the *Book of Leinster* was compiled.

In what is an extremely fantastic narrative that would do justice to present-day *Star Wars* movies, we encounter the Parthalonians, the Fir Bolg, the Tuatha De Danann and the Milesians as they successively find their way into Ireland. And always in the background of these stories there is the evil force of the Formorians. We meet too with heroes of these various legendary peoples like Parthalon himself, Sreng and Eochaid of the Fir Bolg, Lugh, Ogma and Nuadu of the De Danann, and Eremon Eber and Amergin of the Milesians. And then of course there is the one-eyed Balor of the Formorians.

The *Lebor Gabála* sequence of events, played out against the backdrop of kingship at Tara, reads somewhat like real history, and up until only the last one hundred

Page 13B from the *Book of Leinster* contains some of the Invasion Legends. This page clearly shows the ravages that over 900 years of use have wrought on the book's remaining 187 vellum leaves.

At line six in the right column we have the beginning of a poem uttered by the Druid Amergin: '*I seek the land of Ireland. . . .*'

THE BOOK'S HISTORY

1152–61

From internal evidence, such as the naming of kings etc., this is the ten-year period within which the main body of the book was transcribed. The work was chiefly done at Terryglass monastery in north Tipperary, which was founded c. AD548 by St Colum Mac Crimthann. Over 500 years later, having been destroyed by fire, the monastery was abandoned in 1164. The book may at this time have been moved into the safe-keeping of the O'Moores at Oughavail in the homeland of chief scribe Aed's ancestors, the Ui Crimthainn in County Laois, who claimed descent from the High King Crimthann. Material was there added to the volume right up until 1224. Poems in praise of the O'Moores were inserted later still in the fifteenth century.

1324

As part of Celtic Ireland's counter-attack against Norman possessions, the O'Moores of Laois recaptured Oughavail and the rock fortress of Dunamase from powerful representatives of English royalty, the Mortimers, in 1324. For the next 400 years the O'Moore family were protectors of the *Book of Leinster* and made it available to scholars who were creating new compilations of ancient Irish lore during the fourteenth and fifteenth centuries. Both the *Yellow Book of Lecan* (1391) and the *Book of Ballymote* (1410) refer to it as *Lebor Nough na Nuachongbala*.

1447

The O'Moores created a Franciscan monastery at Oughavail and the manuscript may have been housed there in their name.

The Rock of Dunamase in County Laois, a stronghold of the O'Moore's, near where the *Book of Leinster* was preserved for some 400 years at Oughavail.

—— 1502 ——

In a space on folio 37 created by the erasure of previous material, a genealogy of Melaghlin O'Moore was inscribed.

—— 1583 ——

A note on page 259 tells us that in 1583 a scribe named Sean O'Ceirin borrowed the book and that it was still owned by the O'Moores, who had by then lost their lands in the Plantation of Laois and had moved to Ballylea, Co. Kildare.

—— 1627 ——

The portion of the book now in Killiney was with the Franciscans in Donegal where the *Annals of the Four Masters* were soon to be written. For safe-keeping during the time of Cromwell, it was taken to the Franciscan Irish College in Louvain and then on to Rome where it was kept at St Isodore's until it was returned to the Franciscans in Dublin in 1872.

—— 1630 ——

The book was read by Geoffrey Keating for his *History of Ireland*. The main body of the volume was used by the O'Clerys of the Four Masters in 1631 at Lisgoole Franciscan Monastery, Co. Fermanagh, in research for their *Lebor Gabála Erenn*. Seven years later, in 1638, it was back at Ballylea where it was viewed by book collector James Ware. During this period it was the possession of Rory O'Moore, who was to be part of the plot to attack Dublin Castle in the rebellion of 1641.

—— 1700 ——

Antiquarian Edward Lhuyd (who had much to do with publicising the re-discovery of the great tumulus at Newgrange in 1699) acquired what was to him a nameless manuscript from the O'Moores and brought it back with him to England. He also owned the *Seanchus Mór* (the code of ancient Irish law, see Chapter 8) and the *Yellow Book of Lecan* (see Chapter 3). Unlike the latter volume, which he bound, Lhuyd simply made an attempt at ordering and numbering the pages in the *Book of Leinster*. After his death, Lhuyd's library was sold to Sir Thomas Saunders Sebright of Hertfordshire.

—— 1743 ——

The *Book of Leinster* was included in Sebright librarian Thomas Carte's catalogue under the number 122.229 and described as 'A manuscript in Irish characters — ancient hand — vellum in loose sheets tied together.'

—— 1782 ——

At the recommendation of the great Irish orator and parliamentarian Edmund Burke, Sir John Sebright donated the manuscript to Trinity College, Dublin, in 1782, where it was known by its shelf number H.2.18. In 1886 Theophilus O'Flanagan gave it catalogue number 1339 and noted that it was a fragment of either the *Book of Leinster* or the *Book of Glendalough*.

—— 1837 ——

George Petrie agreed with the second of those options when he quoted from H.2.18 in his 1837 book on Tara. Five years later, in 1842, Eugene O'Curry was commissioned by Trinity College to rearrange the pages in preparation for binding. During his work he became convinced that the manuscript was the lost *Book of Leinster* and from about 1845 onwards it has gone by that title.

—— 1880 ——

Just as with *Lebor na hUidre*, Joseph O'Longan created a facsimile of the book for the Royal Irish Academy in 1880. William O'Sullivan's definitive identification of the book with the presumed-lost *Lebor na Nuachongbala* was not made until 1966. Between 1954 and 1983 a definitive six-volume transcript was done for the Royal Irish Academy. In these volumes references are given for sections of the book that have been translated. Just as with *Lebor na hUidre* and the books covered in the next chapter, no complete translation of the *Book of Leinster* has ever been published.

An image of the Druid/poet Amergin.

The Real Book of Glendalough

The *Book of Glendalough* was one of the many names given to the *Book of Leinster*. The real *Book of Glendalough* was declared totally lost by experts for centuris. Instead it lay hidden under another name at Oxford for 150 years. While bound together with another early eleventh-century Irish manuscript in the Bodleian Library there, it became known by the press name Rawlinston B502.

The first part of the composite book, folios 1–12, contains a portion of the *Annals of Tigearnach*, which were copied at Clonmacnoise between the eleventh and fifteenth centuries, with annual notes on Irish and world history from the time of Jonas the Prophet down to 1407. This has marginal notes or glosses written by the same person who wrote the interpolations in *Lebor na hUidre*.

But it is the second part, from folio 13 onwards, which is of most interest here, for in very recent times it has been identified as the real *Book of Glendalough*. It was most probably written at the great monastery of that name sometime around 1126 — just after *Lebor na hUidre* and prior to the *Book of Leinster*. It is a beautifully illuminated text and contains a number of stories relating to Leinster, a very early seventh-century section of the Brehon Laws and a group of 150 biblical poems known as *Saltair na Rann*. Around 1400 this *Book of Glendalough* appears to have been in the possession of the O'Duignan family of Kilronan in Connacht. A member of that family had earlier worked on the *Book of Ballymote* and later another O'Duignan was part of the Four Masters. The *Book of Glendalough* may have been used as a reference by the Four Masters under another name. For some 100 years from 1740–1845 its name the *Book of Glendalough* was mistakenly applied to what we now call the *Book of Leinster*.

The ruins and round tower of Glendalough in County Wicklow, after which beautiful place the *Book of Leinster* was, for a period, named.

CHAPTER III

Scribal Treasures From the West

BOOK *of* BALLYMOTE (1400), GREAT BOOK *of* LECAN (1416), YELLOW BOOK *of* LECAN (1391) *and* BOOK *of* UI MHAINE (O'KELLYS) (1394)

THE BOOK OF BALLYMOTE WAS ONCE EXCHANGED FOR A FORTUNE 'IN MILCH COWS'.

OWNERSHIP OF THE GREAT BOOK OF LECAN WAS THE SUBJECT OF BITTER LEGAL PROCEEDINGS DURING THE REIGN OF WILLIAM AND MARY.

WELSH ANTIQUARIAN EDWARD LHUYD TRAVELLED ACROSS IRELAND TO ACQUIRE THE YELLOW BOOK OF LECAN IN 1700.

THE BOOK OF THE O'KELLYS (UI MHAINE) WAS SOLD IN 1823 FOR ABOUT THE SAME PRICE PAID AT THE TIME FOR ONE OF THE GOLDEN TORQUES OF TARA (£130 STERLING OR PERHAPS €150,000 IN TODAY'S MONEY).

Opposite: List of O'Neill kings from the *Book of Ballymote*.

reguire mc neill. xx. ulm nsi
inbtme port aoubta prior
cumit Ardmhaca puloulle ep
Secunorb irsier porticir mhace vortm
Pui legmierso bup tz oreallatz vepoil
capper m atg lipe ri ravomoc a situ allba
mum ariata vopee puil aiginu ndaripwo
nose pro rmazubail vorb poriee occo corg
gru erou pu riartigelo pro mbaorpru
pic ig gum erou alis eired propate
poetu aire de ionorgmo rure tuerie ull
tbut loggre m neill priceb caffe gup dom
poprig ug me loggre latrmchtaie mc hica
thll molt mc tutg xx bt cotorxeu vair ocu la
chigg cribel mc vall emeave nuppaetg lon
coelbao pig vul apunde mi virir bec mc ve
por eut oeu pfipur tur morttlta eat vili poilt
mc rutg meabatir levul rupur me vo poricu
gemu r loerie mcneill xx bt xx cotorxeu

hese facts give some idea of the value placed upon these great fourteenth- and fifteenth-century compilations and family heirlooms from the west of Ireland. A more touching indication of the esteem in which they were held is to be found in a note added to the *Book of the O'Kellys*. Lamenting the state of this much-consulted volume, it reads: '*Oh! Great book, it is not pleasant for you being handled by everyone.*' The energetic 30-year burst of literary activity between 1390 and 1420 which brought these mighty volumes into being happened within an area still at that time termed Gaelic Ireland — the domain of Irish chieftains who still controlled large sections of land beyond the Shannon in the province of Connacht.

The *Book of Ballymote* was compiled in 1391 at the behest of the Sligo MacDonaghs. Soon afterwards, slightly west of there in the bailiwick of the O'Dowda family, both Books of Lecan were written, and in the land of the O'Kellys, which ran along the Shannon from Roscommon all the way to Clare, the *Book of Ui Mhaine* was created around 1394.

Work on these great books was done by professional historians and scribes, who, in a very different and secular world, carried on the skills and labours that in previous centuries had been the preserve of the Celtic monasteries. When these institutions were either abolished or drastically changed in the Romanised reform movement of the middle twelfth century, there appears to have no longer been any place in them for hereditary scholars like those who produced *Lebor na hUidre* and the *Book of Leinster*.

With the coming of the Normans, there was even less room east of the Shannon for a way of life that was totally Celtic and Gaelic in ethos. Many of the scholarly families, whose roots went back to bards of ancient royal houses, travelled west and brought with them the techniques and knowledge necessary for the continuance of the native literary tradition. Although almost 200 years had elapsed from the time when the *Book of Leinster* had been completed at Terryglass monastery, the tradition was still very much alive in households like those of the Mac Fir Bisigh of Lecan in north Mayo, the O'Duigenans of Roscommon and the Mac Egans of east Galway. All of these families appear to have interplayed in the creation of these four books. The recognisable hands of professional scribes employed by them appear on more than one book and make for a close relationship between the works.

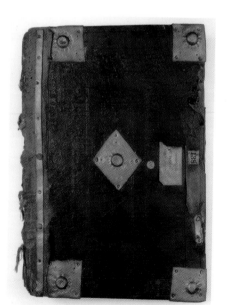

This early cover of the *Great Book of Lecan* is now at the National Museum.

Much of the material in these compilations we have already met in *Lebor na hUidre* and the *Book of Leinster*. But they do expand upon it and each volume adds something new that has become a familiar part of our national lore treasury. At least three of the books were dedicated presentation volumes commissioned and financed by local chiefs who wished to have 'libraries' of well-loved Celtic lore in their houses. On the other hand, the *Great Book of Lecan* was created as a family heirloom of the Mac Fir Bisigh for use in their school of learning.

So long as the Gaelic chiefs of the west controlled their own territories, so too did they continue to maintain their hold on the books as precious treasures. These books were parted with only in the extreme circumstances that prevailed after the Flight of the Earls in 1607. As the story of each book will show, their fate from then on lay very much in the hands of collectors and a variety of Anglo-Irish individuals, who, for their own reasons, took an interest in books that were very much outside the ambit of their inherited culture.

But at the time of their writing, Irish sponsors and patrons of these books were very much in power within their territories. Their right to be so was based on long tradition strongly held, and hence it is not surprising that a good part of the content of these books is taken up with genealogies confirming that tradition. It is impossible to overestimate how important these genealogical texts were in ancient Ireland.[1] This was particularly true at the time that these great books were compiled, during the reigns of Richard II and Henry IV, when English claims over lands west of the Shannon hung in the balance.

As we tell the tale of each book, it will become obvious that all of them followed a somewhat similar road — from the west into Anglo-Irish ownership within the Pale and from there abroad to England or the Continent. Only through the best of good luck and the foresight of some generous individuals were they returned in the nineteenth century to become heirlooms of a nation coming back to life after years of slumber. But the oft-quoted phrase 'The West's Awake' was never more true than in the time that these books were created.

Irish chieftains in the west of Ireland gave their support to the creation of volumes like the *Book of Ballymote* and the *Great Book of Lecan.*

THE BOOK OF BALLYMOTE

amed for the place in Sligo where most of it was compiled, the *Book of Ballymote* is quite a beautiful and very large volume. According to Eugene O'Curry's estimate, the writing would fill 2,500 pages in the *Annals of the Four Masters.*[2]

Its patron was Tomaltach Óg MacDonagh, who was chieftain of the Corann territory in northeast Sligo from 1360 to 1396.

HISTORY OF THE BOOK OF BALLYMOTE

1391–1400

Begun in 1391, the book was probably completed by 1400. A large part of it was written in the magnificent Norman-built keep of Ballymote Castle. But since its main compiler was a young man named Maghnus O'Duigenan, who at that time was a student with the MacEgans of east Galway, some of it was also transcribed in either west Tipperary or east Galway.

Maghnus O'Duigenan was a member of a very learned family of hereditary historians, who had commissions not only for the MacDonaghs but also for their near relatives at Lough Kee, the MacDermots, as well as the O'Farrells of Longford. At a later date Cucogry O'Duigenan was one of the Four Masters, and helped write the famous *Annals of Ireland*. Maghnus lived until 1458, so it is estimated that he was no older than 18 when he toiled along with Donal MacEgan in choosing and compiling the material in this great book. Assisting in its writing at Ballymote were the professional scribes Robert Mac Sheedy and Solamh O'Droma, who also worked on the *Yellow Book of Lecan*.

1522

The MacDonaghs, who were patrons of the work, have been described as a 'warlike sept' who frequently fought with their neighbours, the O'Rourke's, the O'Donnells, the O'Connors and amongst themselves as well. But they were also noted as 'generous patrons of the arts'.[3] They owned the *Book of Ballymote* for just over 100 years before selling it to Aedh Óg O'Donnell for '140 milch cows' in 1522 — a rich return in those times when wealth was still measured in livestock. This price was equal to three times the 'honour price' of MacDonagh himself. It would appear that the transfer of ownership was not all that amicable, for within the

The imposing remains of the MacDonagh fourteenth-century fortress at Ballymote Castle in Sligo, where much of the *Book of Ballymote* was compiled.

book is this comment added on page 401 by the new owner O'Donnell: *'Though the book itself is indeed good; buying a book from MacDonagh is a purchase from a low-class churl.'* Before parting with the book, MacDonagh wrote into it this cryptic but rather bitter note: *'Small is the loss in O'Donnell having forced the book from me for it is a fame of foolishness that has come upon the book.'*[4] Be that as it may, this superb volume was in fact joining two other venerated possessions in the O'Donnell library at that time — the *Book of the Dun Cow* and the *Cathach*.

What happened to the *Book of Ballymote* in the century immediately after its transfer to Donegal is unknown. When the O'Donnells, like so many other of the Earls, were forced to leave the country after the Battle of Kinsale in the early seventeenth century, their wonderful collection of books was dispersed.

A stark nineteenth-century image of Donegal Castle, which was the seat of the O'Donnell chieftains when they had possession of the *Book of Ballymote* and *Lebor na hUidre.*

—— 1620 ——

The next we hear of the *Book of Ballymote* is in 1620 when Duald Mac Fir Bisigh mentions that it was in Dublin — probably in the possession of the then Trinity College Professor and future Protestant Archbishop of Armagh, James Ussher, who was a noted collector of Irish manuscripts.[5]

—— 1710 ——

It was at Trinity College from about 1710 until 1720 when it disappeared for the next 40 years.

—— 1761 ——

It was in the library of a Cork scribe named Michael O'Longan in 1761, and two years later it is known to have been in Dundalk with a Thomas O'Durnin, who was part of a literary family who were friendly with the legendary Chevalier Thomas O'Gorman. The latter had soldiered in France, become known at the court of Louis XV and married the daughter of Count d'Eon, who owned extensive Burgundy vineyards. Having inherited the business, he then became a patron of Irish arts and during frequent visits to Ireland he collected manuscripts. He was partly responsible for the return of the *Book of Lecan* from France and in 1763 he acquired the *Book of Ballymote* from O'Durrin. Then in 1785 he gave it to the newly formed Royal Irish Academy — why not to Trinity where it had previously resided is not known. Sadly, the Chevalier lost his wealth during the French Revolution. Having returned penniless to Ireland, he lived on the generosity of relatives in County Clare until his death at Drumelihy in 1809. He is well remembered through his gift to the Irish nation — the *Book of Ballymote*.

CONTENTS OF THE BOOK OF BALLYMOTE

JUST LIKE OUR TWO previous books in Chapters 1 and 2, this volume contains a huge mass of miscellaneous material collected together in no particular order. At the time that it was compiled, near the end of the fourteenth century, *Lebor na hUidre* was already the proud possession of MacDonagh rivals, the O'Donnells of Donegal. No doubt Tomaltach Óg, for whom *Ballymote* was compiled, wished to have a book that could match or perhaps surpass the *Dun Cow* in terms of genealogical and historical content.

It begins, as is usual with all like compilations of the time, with a copy of the *Lebor Gabála* or the Book of Invasions, and then moves on to include a massive amount of chronological, historical and genealogical tracts in a mixture of both prose and verse. In it, a lengthy attempt was made at tracing the history and pedigrees of all the great families of Ireland and their relationship to the Milesian race. As O'Curry notes, it includes 'the various tribes and families that have branched off in the succession of the ages; so that there scarcely exists an O' or a Mac at the present day who may not find in this book the name of a particular remote ancestor whose name he bears as a surname and from what more ancient line he again was descended'.[6] For septs like the MacDonaghs, who at the end of the troubled fourteenth century were battling against claims on their lands from at home and abroad, this was very important material indeed.

Ballymote also has a much more complete and beautiful *Dindshenchas* than that in the *Book of Leinster*, which gives some superb prose and poetic accounts of the 'sacred places'.

As to ancient lore not yet encountered in either the *Book of Leinster* or *Lebor na hUidre*, there are some interesting tracts:

❖ A copy of the Book of Rights, which delineated the reciprocal rights and tributes due to and from high kings, provincial kings and local chieftains in ancient Ireland.

❖ Following on from that there are some Brehon Law texts that further illuminate knowledge of the old Irish legal system.

A page of *Dindshenchas* (Lore of Sacred Places) material from the *Book of Ballymote*, on which the names of mounds at the Hill of Tara are based.

❖ There is also one of the earliest tracts on the mysterious script of ogham, which was a totally Irish invention and the only form of script used by the writing-shy Celts around the time of St Patrick.

❖ Here too we are brought into the bardic world with a series of tracts on old Irish meter, the many orders and schools of the bards along with the privilege and rewards attached to them, the names of the chief poets of Ireland and the course of instruction used in the schools of the poets.

❖ Our treasury of magical lore is increased through accounts of Conor Mac Nessa, King of Ulster, during the time assigned to the *Táin*, and the accession to kingship of Niall of the Nine Hostages, who was eponymous ancestor of the O'Neill Dynasty that reigned in the name of Tara for almost 900 years.

❖ Here too we find the story of King Cormac Mac Airt's visit to *Tír na nÓg*.

❖ There is also an account of the death of King Crimthainn Mór from whom Aedh, chief scribe of the *Book of Leinster*, claimed ancestry.

❖ There is a more detailed version of the 'Instruction of Princes', which was only briefly touched upon in the *Book of Leinster*. Here there is also a very odd piece that gives an insight into the

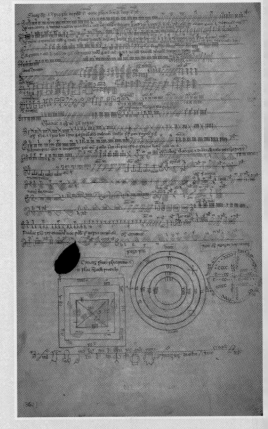

This page from *Ballymote* gives a key to the ogham alphabet.

dichotomy of the king's attitude to women. Cormac was generous to his mistress Cernaith, for whom he is said to have built the first ever mill in Ireland, yet in this instruction to his son Cairbre, we read this in relation to the king's ambivalence toward women:

'I know them but I cannot describe them, their counsel is foolish, they are forgetful of love, most headstrong in their desires, fond of folly, prone to enter rashly into engagements, given to swearing, proud to be asked in marriage, tenacious of enmity, cheerless at the banquet, rejectors of reconciliation, prone to strife, of much garrulity. Until evil be good, until the sun hide its light, until the stars of heaven fall, women will remain as we have stated.'[7] (Not much political correctness there!)

In addition to this strictly native material, the book also gives us uniquely Irish versions of great classical sagas like the Trojan War, the Aeneid, the Wanderings of Ulysses and the exploits of Alexander the Great — stories that at this time found great favour around the campfires of western chieftains like the MacDonaghs. No doubt these tales would have reached Ireland through the interchange between here, England and the Continent by the learned classes and the monks, who travelled to Irish monasteries abroad.

DESCRIPTION OF THE BOOK

The *Book of Ballymote* now has 251 leaves and its 502 pages of vellum text are large and quite legible. They are surrounded by generous margins and have double columns throughout.

Since it was a presentation volume, it appears that the beginning of each major section of the book was initially graced with some elaborate illustrations. Sadly, down the centuries, almost all of these were removed. A complete page drawing of Noah's Ark survives as does an *In Principio*, which scholars feel may have been copied from a now long-lost gospel book. Thankfully we still have just about all of the lovely initial letters that are generously sprinkled throughout the text.

The book remains housed at the Royal Irish Academy, which also possesses Joseph O'Longan's facsimile.

Originally there may have been a number of full-page illuminations in the *Book of Ballymote*. This, the only one surviving, is a depiction of Noah's Ark. A drawing of it was included in P.W. Joyce's *A Social History of Ancient Ireland* (right).

YELLOW BOOK OF LECAN

UNLIKE MANY OTHER books about whose name we can only guess, this one has its title well and truly established right at the beginning of its first section of eight leaves — '*Yellow of Lecan is the name of this book. I am Ciothruadh Mac Taidhg Ruadidh [Mac Fir Bisigh].*' This identifies it as one of the books compiled by the scholarly Mac Fir Bisigh family who had their hereditary historical school at Lecan, Co. Sligo, along the eastern shore of Killala Bay and who were hereditary historians to the powerful O'Dowda chieftains of the Ui Fiachrach territories in Sligo and Mayo.

It is a somewhat eerie experience to now visit that once-revered place of Lecan — only a few hewn stones still clinging to each other remain of the walls that were the Mac Fir Bisigh castle. Nothing remains of the rooms where great books were once compiled and where the learning of ancient Ireland was lovingly preserved.

Just these few remaining stones are a reminder of the Mac Fir Bisigh family's home near Enniscrone, where the *Yellow Book of Lecan* and the *Great Book of Lecan* were written.

But local people point to what may be an even more intimate connection with this great literary family. This is a chair-shaped stone in the field, of which they say: 'The Mac Fir Bisighs sat on that when they did their writing and you will find a round crevice at the edge of it which held their ink.'

Families like the Mac Fir Bisigh were more than historians, for they carried in their genes a deep and precious strain of wisdom and learning that had its roots back in Druidic times. Their aura of sacredness came not from ordination in the Christian Church but from an inheritance, a conviction and a reputation for *knowing* that had its origin back in pre-Christian Ireland. After the coming of Patrick they transformed themselves into Christian men of learning and found refuge within the monastic structures of the Celtic Church. But after the great reform of St Malachy in the twelfth century, there was no longer room for them within Cistercian and Benedictine walls. Herein lay the foundation of new bardic Brehon Law and the historical schools like those of the O'Duignans, MacEgans, O'Dalys and Mac Fir Bisigh.

This large stone in the middle of a field at Lecan is said by locals to have been used by the Mac Fir Bisigh for their writing and they point to a small hole in it as being their ink-well.

The Mac Fir Bisigh

THE MAC FIR BISIGH were proudly descended from the last pagan king of Ireland, Dathí, who was said to have been killed by lightning at the foot of the Alps in AD428. The earliest record we have of them being hereditary historians to the Ui Fiachrach is in the *Annals of the Four Masters*, which note the death of Gilla Isa, 'chief historian of Tir-Fiachrach', in the year 1279. Donagh Mac Fir Bisigh, 'an historian', is recorded as having died in 1376 while the obituary of Firbis Mac Fir Bisigh, 'a learned historian', is recorded in 1397.

This unique family were composers as well as compilers, and they are credited with the origin of the famous and poignant tale 'The Fate of the Children of Lir', which tells of the transformation into swans of four children by a jealous stepmother, 'and they survived in this form for four hundred years on stormy Sea of Moyle until their final rescue when the spell has run out and they are returned to human form at the bay of Erris in County Mayo'. One wonders if the Sea of Moyle was not inspired by the imaginings of a Mac Fir Bisigh looking out from his vantage point at Lecan onto the sometimes equally stormy Moy estuary as it churns into the Atlantic at Killala Bay.

Gilla Isa Mac Fir Bisigh, the chief compiler of both the *Yellow Book of Lecan* and the *Great Book of Lecan*, was a descendant of the Gilla Iosa of 1279 and a son of Donnchadh Mór Mac Fir Bisigh. Thus he was a direct ancestor of the legendary Dudley (or Duald) Mac Fir Bisigh, who was the last of the line and sadly died by murder in 1670 when he intervened to save a young girl from being molested by a violent drunkard named Crofton. Deprived of his family lands, he lived most of his life in poverty and yet was responsible for some brilliant genealogical, legal and historical tracts.

With patronage from Rory Mac Donall O'Dowda, Gilla Iosa Mac Fir Bisigh and his son Tomas Cam began work on the *Yellow Book of Lecan* in 1391. It was intended both as a prize possession of the O'Dowdas and also as a textbook for the Mac Fir Bisigh school at Lecan. With the assistance of professional scribe Solamh O'Droma, who also worked on the *Book of Ballymote*, the main body of the volume was completed by 1420. However, as late as 1592 some further material was added. Not all the writing took place in Lecan, for, according to internal evidence within the book itself, parts of it were transcribed in Cork, Tipperary and Galway.

The original *Yellow Book of Lecan* appears to have had 165 leaves. But, as we mentioned, it accumulated many more later on and now contains 236 leaves of very varied material. It remained with the Mac Fir Bisigh family until around 1670 when the hard-pressed Duald transferred ownership to one of his Galway students. Around 1699 it became the possession of Welsh collector Edward Lhuyd. After his death, Lhuyd's collection was sold to Sir Thomas Sebright in 1715. His son Sir John Sebright bequeathed the *Book of Leinster*, the *Yellow Book of Lecan* and a copy of the *Seanchus Mór* to Trinity College in 1786.

CONTENTS OF THE YELLOW BOOK OF LECAN

ACCORDING TO EUGENE O'CURRY, the contents of its over 500 pages of writing would fill 2000 pages in the *Annals of the Four Masters*. It is written in either two or three columns per page and references to it are made according to the numbered lines within numbered columns. In all, it contains 100 items in prose and poetry that include civil and ecclesiastical history along with a great variety of legendary lore. It repeats a number of pieces already covered in our three previous books, including a more complete version of the *Táin*, an account of the Battle of Magh Rath in County Down, the Battle of Magh Leana of AD718, the Battle of Dunbolg, Co. Wicklow, in which King of Tara Aedh Mac Ainmire died in AD594. There is also a repeat of the fateful story of King Conaire's death in 'Da Derga's Hostel'. The voyage of Maelduin on the Atlantic is recorded once more, along with some less dramatic Voyage stories, like that of Snedgus. Cormac's adventures in the Land of Promise are recounted once more.

Among the new items we meet there are further stories relating to Fionn Mac Cumhaill, more Brehon Law material, and poems about Tara, along with a plan of the legendary banqueting hall there.

Here as well we find a unique story about the 'cursing' of Tara. Following a bitter disagreement between the sixth-century King of Tara, Dermot Mac Fergus Cerbaill, and St Ruadhan of Lorrha, the saint and his companions descended on Tara, where they fasted and rang their bells against Dermot, declaring that no king would ever reign in Tara again.

There is also a fantastic story about another sixth-century King of Tara, Muirchertach Mac Erca, and his disastrous confrontation with a Druidess named Sin. She wound up drowning him in a vat of wine at his fortress of Cletty by the banks of the Boyne, near present-day Bective.

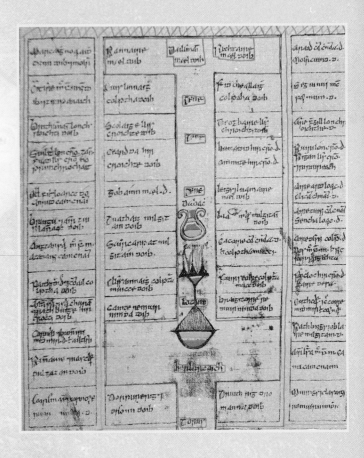

A facsimile of the plan of the Banqueting Hall at Tara as found in the *Yellow Book of Lecan*.

The expulsion of the Deisi tribe from Tara is recounted, along with further stories about Conor Mac Nessa, King of Ulster. An account of the inter-regal strife that ended in the destruction of the royal Leinster site of Dind Righ is here. And reflecting some of the more widespread interest of the time, stories of Greek and Roman heroes are included as well.

To be found at the beginning of the book are poems relating to the O'Donnells of Donegal, the O'Connors of Sligo and Galway, and the O'Kelly's of Ui Mhaine, which were not added to the book until the late sixteenth century. But the Ui Mhaine were also immortalised in their own book and we treat of that next.

'The Cursing of Tara' from the *Yellow Book of Lecan*. Starting with the letter F in the lower left column, it tells the story of the saints and bishops from the sixth century coming to Tara and fasting against the high king.

THE LEBOR UI MHAINE OR
BOOK OF THE O'KELLYS

HE *LEBOR UI MHAINE* IS another volume that miraculously survived years of turmoil during the late Middle Ages in Ireland and emerged from the west to tell us more about our past and what shaped us into what we are. Exemplifying how one of these great books fared with time, the *Lebor Ui Mhaine* is now less than half the size it was when first completed around 1394. At that time it possessed 368 large vellum leaves. By 1500 it had lost 60 of these and as it is today at the Royal Irish Academy it is down to just 157 pages. A further four leaves got separated off while it was in England and these are now housed at the British Library. No wonder one reader of the book wrote his lament into its pages: '*Oh Great Book, it is not pleasant for you being handled by everyone.*'

The O'Kellys, for whom this compilation was created by six professional scribes, were at that time (near the end of the fourteenth century) still in control of a huge strip of land along the western shore of the Shannon. At its greatest extent in pre-Norman times, this territory of Ui Mhaine had reached all the way from Roscommon down to the tip of Lough Derg in County Clare, comprising at least 1,000 square miles. If you stand in the graveyard of Clonmacnoise and gaze westwards across the Shannon you will be looking into the heart of the ancient territory called Ui Mhaine — flat land beautifully extending west into the haze of the Slieve Aughty Mountains.[8]

The chieftains of this vast territory traced their ancestry back almost one thousand years to around AD437, when Maine Mór from the royal line of Emain Macha in Ulster took control of a section of sword land west of the Shannon near Lough Ree. His descendants extended it north and south from there along the great river. Much later, in the eleventh century, they took the name O'Kelly, from Cellagh, the twelfth prince of Ui Mhaine, whose son Tadgh Mór fought and died with Brian Boru at the Battle of Clontarf.

Ui Mhaine chieftains became hereditary marshals to the kings of Connacht and, despite Norman incursions and the efforts of Dublin Castle to extend its power across the Shannon, in 1394, when this book was written, they still held power under Brehon Law over a good section of this territory. In fact it was not until 1585 that they were said to have submitted to the British Crown, promising 'to hence forth behave themselves like good subjects and bring up their children after the English fashion and in the use of the English tongue'.[9] It is doubtful that they kept that promise for very long, since down the centuries the O'Kellys remained faithful to the Irish cause. They were part of the revolution in 1641, they fought with James II at the Battle of the Boyne and they were with Patrick Sarsfield in his defence of Limerick in 1690. An O'Kelly was Revolutionary Emissary to the USA in 1919 and from 1959 to 1969 Sean T. O'Kelly was the second President of the Irish Republic.

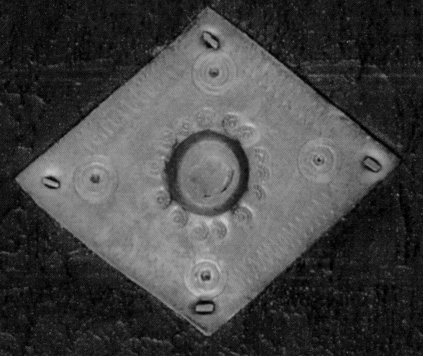

138

PRESENTED BY

Dr Petrie.

138

376.

CONTENTS OF THE BOOK OF THE O'KELLYS

THE BOOK WAS MOST probably begun as a memorial to a great chieftain of Ui Mhaine, William O'Kelly, who died in 1375. He was reputed to have been a generous supporter of the arts, and in the *Annals of Clonmacnoise* it is recorded that he once invited '*all the Irish Poets, Brehons, Bards, Harpers, Gamesters, Jesters and others of their kind*' to his house for a Christmas celebration (year 1351). A further occasion for having the *Lebor Ui Mhaine* written was in fact the elevation of one Muircheartach O'Kelly to the powerful Archbishopric of Tuam. He had formerly been Bishop of Clonfert from 1378 to 1394 and in that latter year took the prestigious Tuam seat. Thus the book was intended as a celebration of both the old Gaelic heritage and of the O'Kelly place in it. For example, a full 70 pages are given over to tracing their own family's genealogical lines. Once again we cannot overemphasise the importance of this material within a community that was struggling with its neighbours over territorial rights while at the same time striving to retain their very identity within an increasingly anglicised Ireland. At the very time the book was being written, Malachy O'Kelly, who had succeeded as chieftain, was in contention with the Anglo-Irish Earl of Ormond over a piece of territory to which his family claimed ownership.

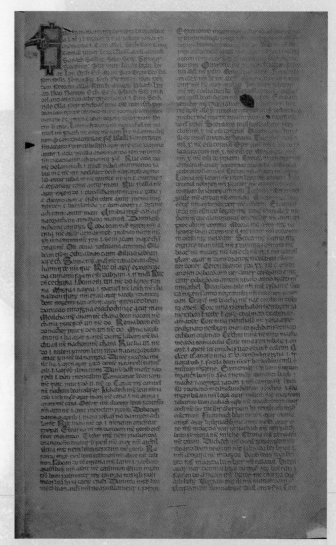

Page from the *Book of Ui Mhaine*, which was created for presentation to the Bishop of Tuam. This page includes part of the tract *Banshenchas*, which is a chronicle of famous women. It begins with the words '*Eva Bean Ahaim*' – Eve the wife of Adam.

But this book concentrates not just on the Connacht genealogies, rather it extends to all four provinces and is an important source for histories of those areas as well. Given the context in which it was written, it is not surprising then that *Ui Mhaine* also contains a large segment of the Book of Rights, which runs to some 20 pages, followed by another section on the Roll of Kings.

The book leans more towards historical than legendary material. Thus it has long tracts on Ireland's story and some pages of what might be called pseudo-history, like the story of St Patrick's tooth, a shrine dating from the twelfth century which was used for cures.

Ui Mhaine adds greatly to the volume of *Dindshenchas* poems and prose about how certain places were named and the events that caused them to be so designated.

Once again it provides a copy of the *Banshenchas* or the history of famous Irish women from ancient times. One has to feel that at some time during this very active period in Irish literature a woman or group of women demanded some equal treatment on the pages of these vellum manuscripts of the late fourteenth and early fifteenth centuries. In fact, this list of 'famous women' and the 'wives of famous men' covers no less than 18 tightly knit columns on pages 95 to 105.

Over 15 pages are taken up with secular poetry on a variety of subjects. Also included is a long poem in praise of the O'Kellys, which may have been composed after William O'Kelly's legendary Christmas party in 1351 for the poets and musicians of Ireland.

HISTORY OF THE
THE BOOK OF THE O'KELLY'S

1100

In the top to bottom reform of the Irish Church, which so painfully took place in the twelfth century, the creation of just four Archbishoprics was an important feature. In this division of ecclesiastical powers on the island, Tuam stood second only to the Prime See of Armagh and on equal footing with both Dublin and Cashel. At the time that the *Book of Ui Mhaine* was compiled, the chair at Tuam was vacant and the most likely candidate to fill it was the then Bishop of Clonfert, Muircheartach Ua Ceallaigh. To have an O'Kelly in line for this hugely important post was not taken lightly by leaders of the tribe. It is thought that one of the ways in which they celebrated was through the creation of this massive volume highlighting the O'Kelly place in Irish history for presentation to Muircheartach at the time of his elevation.

At the conclusion of his section of the work, one scribe, Faolan Mac nGhabhann na Sceal, included this cautionary note: '*I wrote this caidirne for my lord, friend and companion Muircheartach and I plead with him not to part with it.*' He may have heeded the plea all right but in later years the O'Kellys appear to have had a difficult time holding on to this literary treasure.

1394

We can assume that the *Book of Ui Mhaine* was finished at the time that Muircheartach Ua Ceallaigh was installed as Archbishop of Tuam in 1394. It appears to have remained in O'Kelly control for the next fifty years or so, but at that time a note added on folio 3 indicates that it was then the possession of one Mael Muire ua Uiginn, a learned man of Connacht, who died in 1488. This note also tells us that at that time it still had 368 leaves.

1620

It is next heard of in 1620 when Dublin historian Sir James Ware had access to it and employed that hero of Irish learning, Duald Mac Fir Bisigh, to create a list of the book's contents. The great Duald's signature is to be found on page 571. Later in that century it was somehow back into O'Kelly hands, for on folio 77 it tells us that Walter O'Kelly then owned it.

—— 1754-1820 ——

A Loughlen O'Kelly of Loughrea had it in 1754, but after that, like so many other of the great books of Ireland, it made its way across the Irish Sea and by 1820 it was owned by book collector Sir William Betham. He sold it for £150 sterling to the library of the Duke of Buckinghamshire at Stowe where it was housed side by side with the beautiful *Stowe Missal*.

—— 1849-1885 ——

Lord Ashburnham bought the manuscripts from the Stowe Library in 1849. The Irish section of that massive collection was purchased by the British Government in 1883 and two years later, as part of that consignment, the *Book of Ui Mhaine* was handed over to the Royal Irish Academy, which had a photographic facsimile made. It can now also be viewed on the DCU website www.isos.dcu.ie.

THE GREAT BOOK OF LECAN

AVING A MUCH MORE dramatic history than its sister book from the Mac Fir Bisigh school was what is called the *Great Book of Lecan*, which dates from around 1416. It made its way to Trinity College, Dublin, was spirited away from there, possibly by King James II, and ended up in France, where it became the subject of litigation between two claimants to ownership.

Unlike either *Ballymote* or the *Yellow Book of Lecan*, which were produced at the behest of local chieftains, this compilation appears to have been written specifically as a reference book for the Mac Fir Bisigh school, for on folio 32 is found this note: '*A prayer for Mac Firbisich, who wrote this book as an heirloom for all who will come after him for ever and in the time of Ruaidri Ua Dubda it was written.*' The Ruaidri here mentioned died in 1417; so the usual date put on the book is 1416. Just as with the *Yellow Book of Lecan*, Gilla Iosa is again credited with being the main scribe, but this time he was assisted by Murchadh Riahach O Cuindlis, who worked in Munster, and Udhlamh O Cuirnin, who contributed the best copy of the *Lebor Gabála* that exists.

The book is known to have remained at Lecan until at least 1550. When next mentioned in 1612 it was in the hands of Dublin Castle bureaucracy as the possession of one Henry Perse, who was Secretary to the Lord Deputy of Ireland, Sir Arthur Chichester. Some time after that, it was acquired by Reformation Archbishop of Armagh and inveterate book collector James Ussher. He is known to have loaned it to Westmeath historian Conall Mageoghegan in 1636.

But by 1688 the book was in the library of Trinity College and listed in their catalogue. Sadly, just 14 years later, *Lecan* was included among a list of missing books published by the College in 1702.[10] In the intervening years, during the latter part of the Williamite wars, Trinity was used by King James as a residence for himself and a billet for his army. As a natural result of this fact, the book's disappearance has traditionally been linked to the fleeing king. Only 60 years after the event, this tradition was so firmly established that it found its way into the great Abbe Mac Geoghegan's *History of Ireland*, published in Paris in 1758: 'The late king of England, James II, had a large manuscript volume in folio called *Leaver Lecan* taken from the Library of Trinity College Dublin.'[11] And this belief stood for the next 200 years or so.

The Irish College in Paris where the *Great Book of Lecan* resided prior to its being generously returned to Ireland in the late eighteenth century.

More recently the certitude of that statement has been called into question but has never been definitively disproved. Whether in the possession of King James as he fled Ireland after the Battle of the Boyne or in the hands of some person close to him we do not know for certain, but we do know that a major part of the *Great Book of Lecan* at that time made its way to France, and there it soon became the subject of court proceedings between two rival claimants to its ownership, who had connections with the royal court of the English at St Germain.

The opening nine folios were separated from the main body of the volume at this time. They either stayed at Trinity or became part of the batch of Irish manuscripts that Edward Lhuyd brought out of Ireland in 1700. This section of genealogical material was re-discovered in 1845 by Eugene O'Curry when he was working at Trinity on the *Book of Leinster*. They were at that time stored along with the Sebright Collection, which included the *Yellow Book of Lecan*.

King James II died at St Germain in 1701 and it is in that place that the next piece of the book's story unfolds. Sometime prior to 1703 a Limerick man, Sir John Fitzgerald, who had been an officer in the king's army, sold the book to an expatriot from Athlone named James Terry, who styled himself 'The Irish Herald' at the court of St Germain. In later discovered letters he valued the book at £500 sterling but it is doubtful that he paid that amount for it. There is also doubt as to whether he took possession of the book at the time of sale. At least we know that very soon afterward it was still in the care of Fitzgerald, who in turn loaned it to a relative of Terry by the name of Doctor Matthew Kennedy. He used it as a source when writing his *Dessertion of the Royal Family of the Stuarts*.

It may be that Kennedy felt that he too had bought the book, for when asked to give it up by Terry, he solidly refused and at this point a bitter legal wrangle between the two men began. Both Terry and Kennedy wrote to Queen Mary asking her to set up a court of distinguished persons, who would adjudicate on the matter of ownership.

Whatever happened next we do not know, but in July of 1705 James Terry wrote a letter to the Duke of Perth containing this cryptic sentence: 'I have been ordered by the Vice-Chamberlain not to goe to court, upon account of my title or noe title to Lecan an Irish book.'[12] Students of the strange case surmise that Terry got his way and the matter did not go to court. He died soon afterwards and somehow, perhaps through the good offices of Fitzgerald, the book was turned over to the Irish College of the Lombards in Paris. Its eventual return to Ireland near the end of the eighteenth century was brought about through the good efforts of both the Royal Dublin Society (RDS), which had been in existence since 1731, and the newly founded Royal Irish Academy, which was established in 1785.

It was in 1772 that the RDS initiated a strenuous effort to recover some of Ireland's exiled manuscripts by appointing a committee 'to enquire into the ancient state of arts, literature, and other antiquities of this Kingdom'. None other than Chevalier O'Gorman, whom we mentioned as the saviour of the *Book of Ballymote*, was appointed by this new committee 'to apply to various colleagues and learned institutions in France for copies of any manuscripts and records illustrative of the history and antiquities of Ireland'.[13] The Chevalier did make contact with the Irish College in Paris and this resulted in the superiors there convening a meeting of 'all persons connected with Ireland' on March 11, 1773. Out of that meeting came the promise of a transcript of *Lecan* but not the desired return of the book itself to Ireland.

There is no record of the promised transcript ever having been delivered either, and there matters stood for the next ten years or so. Then in the mid-1780s the Royal Irish Academy came into being. Many of those involved in its creation, like Colonel Charles Vallancey and William Conyngham, were also high-ranking

Colonel Charles Vallancey, who played a major role in negotiations to have the *Great Book of Lecan* returned to Ireland and to the Royal Irish Academy in 1787.

members of the RDS and thus they brought with them into the new organisation the desire to complete the projects begun by the RDS Antiquarian Committee back in 1772. A prime mover in a new effort to retrieve *Lecan* was Vallancey, who was named Vice-President of the RDS in 1799. He was in Paris at the time that crucial negotiations for the book's return took place in 1787. In May of that year he wrote to the treasurer of the Royal Irish Academy, William Conyngham, recommending a request for the book from the Academy to Abbe Charles Kearney, who was then rector of the Irish College in Paris. Following on from this, Vallancey was commissioned by the Academy to 'take whatever steps were necessary for the book's return'. What these steps were we do not know, but it is certain that he asked the British Ambassador at the Court of Versailles to intervene. A certain Chevalier O'Reilly was also very positively involved. One way or another, the record shows that on September 10, 1787 the *Great Book of Lecan* was officially presented to the Royal Irish Academy, and at a meeting of Council on that day a resolution was passed that a letter of sincere thanks from the Academy should be sent to Abbe Kearney at the Irish College for its safe return. From a little field by the Bay of Killala by a very circuitous route to a beautiful library in the heart of Dublin, *Lecan* was home.

The Royal Irish Academy on Dawson Street, Dublin, founded in the late eighteenth century and now a rich repository for ancient Irish manuscripts like the *Book of Ballymote* and the *Great Book of Lecan*.

No doubt religious feelings at the time influenced the decision to have the book presented to the newly formed Academy rather than to Trinity College, where it had previously resided and where it could eventually have been reunited with its first nine folios. But an Irish solution to an Irish problem had been forged and thus it stands.

Lecan escaped Paris in the nick of time, for just two years after its return to Ireland the library of the Irish College was broken up during the French Revolution. Like so many other Irish books, *Lecan* could well have been lost forever. The great antiquarian Owen Connellan, who did the first ever English translation of the latter part of the *Annals of the Four Masters* and who has been termed 'one of the last representatives of traditional Gaelic scholarship', was asked by Queen Victoria to create a transcript of the *Great Book of Lecan* for the Royal Library at Windsor in the 1850s. Around the same time Eugene O'Curry did an extensive outline of its contents for the Royal Irish Academy.

THE CONTENTS OF THE GREAT BOOK OF LECAN

SOME PIECES ARE presumed missing from the text, but as it now stands the *Great Book of Lecan* has 604 pages on 302 A4-sized vellum leaves, of which 293 are at the Royal Irish Academy, while the nine discovered by Eugene O'Curry are still at Trinity College. Since it was intended as a family book of the Mac Fir Bisigh and not as a presentation volume, the book is rather plain-looking. But it is very tastefully written in two columns per page, which are just slightly decorated with initials in vermilion and yellow. As indicated within the text itself, this illumination was done by chief scribe Mac Gilla Iosa himself. One can imagine him of a late evening looking out on peaceful Killala Bay writing this rather poignant commentary about his work on folio 162: *'Tonight is the eve of Sunday, and an end has been made of the colouring of all this book, and there is great war in Connacht, it is a fortnight from tonight to the first of August (Lugnusad) Mac Firbisigh scripsit.'*

In terms of general content *Lecan* is very similar to the *Book of Ballymote* and one can imagine some form of co-operation between the Mac Fir Bisigh and their near neighbours, the O'Duignans, in its creation. However, within it, the various genealogical, historical and topographical tracts of *Ballymote* are greatly expanded. It includes a unique section on the 'five great roads of ancient Ireland', which Petrie extensively used in his book on Tara. Two copies of the *Lebor Gabála Érenn* are included and the second of them, done by Adhamh Ó Cuirrin, is thought to be the most perfect in existence.

Its genealogies are among the best sources for students of both the history and geography of ancient Ireland. People who today attempt to piece together their Irish roots are often dependent on this book for their basic material. Not surprisingly, it includes a large section on the O'Dowds and the Ui Fiachrach territory of west Sligo. As part of this, there is a fascinating description of the Mac Fir Bisigh involvement in the inauguration ceremony of the O'Dowda chieftains. Their prominent role gives some indication of the power and influence vested in families that carried on the bardic tradition as hereditary poets and historians. Here is a brief summary of the role played by the Mac Fir Bisigh in the inauguration ceremony of the O'Dowda chieftains:

'The O'Dowda was not to drink until 'the poet' Mac Firbisigh had drunk from the celebration cup. And it was never right to call the new chieftain 'The O'Dowda' until the Mac Fir Bisigh first called his name and carried the body of the wand over him. And every king of the men of Fiachra that shall not be thus proclaimed shall have shortness of life and his seed and generation shall not be illustrious and he shall never see the Kingdom of God.'[14]

This inauguration ceremony contains a delightful mixture of Gaelic Druidic taboos and the salvation beliefs of Christianity, showing that right up until the 1400s remembrance of the 'old ways' was still very much alive.

This dichotomy and yearning for things past still invests life in a good part of Ireland today and it is at the heart of what makes this people at the edge of the Atlantic just that bit different from the rest of Europe. We return to this theme in the next chapter where we are transported back to the third century and the tales associated with Fionn Mac Cumhaill.

A colourful page of Dindshenchas (Lore of Sacred Places) poems from the *Great Book of Lecan*.

CHAPTER IV

Finding Fionn Mac Cumhaill

THE BOOK
of
LISMORE
(1480)

L OST AND GNAWED BY RATS INSIDE A CASTLE WALL,

FOUND IN 1814 ONLY TO THEN BE PILLAGED OF ITS

PAGES, WHAT IS LEFT OF THE BOOK OF LISMORE IS

STILL A UNIQUE MONUMENT FROM MEDIEVAL IRELAND AND

CONTAINS THE MOST ANCIENT DETAILED NARRATIVE WE HAVE

ABOUT FIONN MAC CUMHAILL AND THE FIANNA.

Opposite: A page from sister book to *Lismore*, the fifteenth-century *Book of Fermoy*.

abuın dechınaó ʒnoana· no oıa maʒıaʒ oıꞃʒmala· mıcheıſ no
Atu ꞃıam ınꞃıacht uaım· aʒell ꞃꞇa maċenoum· nochanꝼuıl ı
aꞃ mo oam· aʒell no tꞃʒan aoenam· ı̇·

Sıo aʒ oʒam aꞃꞃoana· oa chaó ċaꞃ chꞃo eoala· anꞇʒ no
ꞇaꞃaꞃceaꞇo· maꞃ uꞇʒıeꞃ aꞃe nach aꞃꞃꞃeaın· ı̇·

Taꞃꞃu olʒ ealuóaın oʒ· ʒıo ole beꞃꞃaın abuıoe· ınꝼeꞇꞃe me an
ꝼlaꞇ oam· oꞃꞇꞃmaó anꞇʒ oa ꞇaꞃꞃꞃao· ı̇· Aunʒ· aꞃꞃ ꞃe no cuaıo caıꞃ
ach oam aꞃ oouʒ leam· buʒa ꞃe oꞃa maıꞃoꞇſꞇꞃo· ʒıo ꞃuaıl oꞃe
oca ıꞇꞃꞃꞃuıl uan· ꞃeſoa aꞃooꞃmaꞃo ꞃꞃꞃꞃoʒ oua· oeachınaó aꞃleꞃo
ꞃꞃꞃo ꞃo ouan aꞃ ꞃa oeꞃ ꞃouanꞇꞃıb· ı̇· ꞃꞇ4 oeachınaó ꞃa oenam
ı̇ achꞃꞃꞃaʒa aꞃooꞇʒ oıꞃ· ʒan ınꞃꞃꞃꞃaın· oꞃꞃꞃoꞃꞃʒ· aeıꞃ no ʒebꞇ4 oꞇʒul
ꞃe ꞃꞃꞃꞃꞃa ꞃſ me aınꞃꞃʒ· oꞃa oa oꞃꞃınaó ma oꞃchınaꞃo· naꞃeıch ꞃa caꞃꞃ
Alo anꝼꞇꞇꞃʒıll aꞃꞃꞃꞃꞃꞇꞃl· ı̇· ıꞃ̇ꞃ· maꞃ oꞃ̇aꞃ ꞃe ꞃen ʒan ꞃaꞃꞃꞇꞃꞃ
no chaó ꞃꞃꞃꞃoın ꞃuꞇꞃo· oabꞃꞃꞃ anaꞃꞃʒe oꞃuın· aꞇa anbaꞃ ꞃebel ʒan
ʒaꞃꞇa uꞃꞃabuıo· ʒıo meꞃꞃꞃe amoꞇꞃuʒuo· aꞃꞃeꞃ ꞃe ꞇꞇb ʒe cꞃꞃꞃ
aʒach oen anaꞃ· ı̇· oaꞇʒ· ınbeachꞇ lʒ oıꞃ aʒ oeaʒoꞃꞃ·
aꞇꞃaꞃ anꞇꞃꞃ aꞃchıo· buꞃꞃba moꞃ nach moꞇꞃꞃꞇꞃꞃ· ꞃꞃao aꞃꞃꞃ ooı
ꞃ ꞃꞃꞃꞃ ꞃꞃꞃꞃ aınach· ınꞇꞃꞃꞇſbeo aꞃnaınaꞃꞃꞇch· eꞃꞇch ʒach ꞇꞃꞃ leı
oobꞃꞃaın oaıo cohaꞃꞃꞃʒlc· ı̇· achꞃꞃaꞃ aꞃꞃaꞃ aꞃchınela·
ꞃꞃoe aꞃꞃꞃın ʒuꞃꞃ· theꞃa ꞃa anꞃꞃe moꞃ muꞃꞃe· la anbuaꞇꞃ buꞃ achlaꞃ
ꞃaobuın moꞃoe· ꞇochꞇ anꞇan ꞃaꞇꞃmoꞇoe· ınꝼꞃꞇa ꞃꞃʒa ꞃa naꞃꞃ

THE LEGEND OF FIONN MAC CUMHAILL

Before looking at the history and contents of the *Book of Lismore*, let us concentrate for a time on the fame of Fionn Mac Cumhaill, whose exploits take up a full quarter of this fifteenth-century volume's 197 folia.

While always the most popular heroic figure in Irish saga literature, Fionn Mac Cumhaill is like the Pimpernel of our ancient lore. Unlike Cúchulainn, whose story is well told in books like *Lebor na hUidre*, the *Book of Leinster* and the *Book of Lecan*, one has to seek out Fionn here and there throughout the preserved Celtic writings not only here in Ireland but abroad as well.

There are in fact two strands to his lore. One of these is entirely mythological, in which Fionn is portrayed as a magnificent giant capable of prodigious feats associated with many geographical features throughout the land — it was he who scooped out a fistful of earth to form a lake and it was also he who created the Giant's Causeway as he flung huge rocks into the Irish sea in his bid to reach Scotland. He had the gift of wisdom in a magic tooth and could look far into the future to foresee events like the arrival of the Danes or the actions of the infamous twelfth-century Leinster king, Dermot Mac Murrough.

The other persona of Fionn is pseudo-historical, in which he is portrayed as a third-century leader of the Fianna band who protected Ireland's shores from invasion during the reign of Cormac Mac Airt. At the time that these stories blossomed in the fifth and sixth centuries, Ireland was still in a twilight zone between the old

Fionn Mac Cumhaill – the hero of the Finian Cycle of Tales. One of many Irish landscape features intertwined with the legends of Fionn Mac Cumhaill is the Giant's Causeway on the coast of Antrim. He is said to have flung the huge rocks into the ocean during his bid to reach Scotland

Druidic religion and Christianity. In this milieu Fionn was a kind of incarnation god-man figure who combined in his person Otherworld magic and the heroic prowess of a human warrior.

Both as mythology and as pseudo-history, Finian lore appears to have permeated the population of this island during the post-Patrician centuries. It reached beyond our shores as well with the Dalriada colonisers of Scotland, where, for hundreds of years, stories about Fionn were the common lore of Highland folk. And it is from material later written down by the Scots that a good deal of what we associate with this hero of the past was transmitted back to us.

Witness the number of poems about Fionn (or Fingal as he was known there) collected in the Gaelic Scottish Highlands by James Macpherson as late as 1760. In addition, a large number of verses about him gleaned from the Tay Valley were included in the sixteenth-century *Book of the Dean of Lismore*.

This latter compilation, which is not to be confused with our own *Book of Lismore*, was written around 1540 by two brothers, James and Duncan Macgregor from Perthshire. Among the many verses in this compilation attributed to Fionn's son Oisín we find this:

'I've seen the household of Fionn,
No men were they of coward race,
I saw by my side a vision,
Of the hero's household yesterday.'[1]

And in another of its poems Fionn is found communing with nature:

'Sweet is man's voice in the land of gold
Sweet the sounds the birds produce,
Sweet the murmur of the crane,
Sweet the sound of waves at Bundatreor,
Sweet the murmuring of the wind,
Sweet sounds of cuckoo at Cas-s Choin
How soft and pleasing shines the sun,
Sweet the blackbird sings his song.'[2]

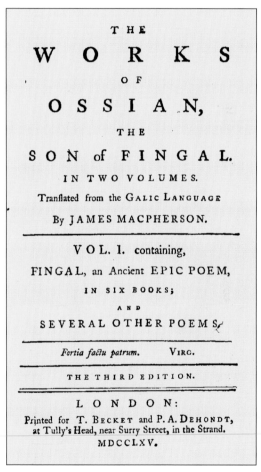

THE
W O R K S
OF
O S S I A N,
THE
SON of FINGAL.
IN TWO VOLUMES.
Tranſlated from the GALIC LANGUAGE
By JAMES MACPHERSON.

VOL. 1. containing,
FINGAL, an Ancient EPIC POEM,
IN SIX BOOKS;
AND
SEVERAL OTHER POEMS.

Fortia faƈtu patrum. VIRG.

THE THIRD EDITION.

LONDON:
Printed for T. BECKET and P. A. DEHONDT,
at Tully's Head, near Surry Street, in the Strand.
MDCCLXV.

The Ossianic and Finian lore which made its way to the Scottish highlands is preserved in two volumes. The *Book of the Dean of Lismore* (sixteenth century) and *The Works of Oisín* (eighteenth century), of which this is the title page.

James Macpherson, in his 1760 two-volume publication *The Works of Ossian the Son of Fingal*, certainly kept the Finian lore alive, not only in Scotland but far beyond these islands in Europe and America right into the eighteenth century. In one of his collected poems he thus depicts the hero Fionn in action:

'Fingal heard the sound and took his father's spear,
His steps were before us on the heath,
He spoke the words of woe.
I hear the noise of battle: and Oscar is alone.
Rise ye sons of Morven and join the hero's sword.'[3]

Oisín and Niamh on their way to Tír na nÓg: a mural by Bob Cathail in the Bradan Feasa Restaurant, Ventry.

More than a century earlier than Macpherson, some of the Irish exiles that followed the Flight of the Earls onto the Continent brought Finian lore with them. In 1626 some of it was published at Louvain in a book of poems called *Duanaire Finn*. Again depicting the warrior band's love of nature, one of these verses beautifully begins:

'The voice of the beagle on Knocknaree — dear to me the hill round which it sounds
Often we held fenian feasts between the mountain and the sea.'[4]

In both the Scottish and Belgian material it is obvious that Finian lore was for centuries the stuff of common entertainment among the Irish at home and abroad. But, oddly enough, mentions of Fionn are very scarce in our earliest books of ancient lore. *Lebor na hUidre* includes just one story about him in its varied contents — that in which Mongan is said to be another persona of *Find mac Cumaill* (f. 133). There are also vague allusions to him in a tract called 'The Causes of the Battle of Knock'. The *Book of Leinster* has four tales about Fionn plus a number of poems attributed either to him, his son Oisín or his companion Caoilte.

Now this shortage of material in these two great books does not at all mean that Fionn and his legends were unknown at the time that *Lebor na hUidre* and the *Book of Leinster* were compiled in the eleventh and twelfth centuries. It simply means that these books were aiming at preserving the more aristocratic of the tales, like those about Cúchulainn, which were in danger of being lost forever. The compilers of these works may have felt that Finian lore was so well known among the vassal classes that there was no danger of its ever dying out and therefore there was no need to find space for it in their compilations. They were right in that assumption, since the popularity of Finian and Ossianic lore continues right up until our own time. Some of it was not actually composed until the early eighteenth century. Then, in the late nineteenth century, through translations published by people like P. W. Joyce, T. W. Rolleston and Lady Gregory, Fionn stories achieved a new impetus once more.

Margaret Clarke's image of St Patrick as an old man suits the story of his meeting up with the aged Oisín to review the great Ossianic tales.

But it is all the way back to the late twelfth century that we must go for the most basic source of Fionn lore available to all of these writers. For it was then that an unnamed author created a unique tract called *The Colloquy of the Ancients*. This author drew together some 200 Finian episodes into a masterful narrative which has as its main theme the meeting of ancient pagan Ireland with the Christianity of St Patrick. The oldest, most complete text of this unique tract now extant is to be found in the fifteenth-century *Book of Lismore*. If fully transcribed, it would take up over 200 pages of a printed volume like this one.

Playing a magic trick with the ages, the author of the *Colloquy* has the leaders of the Fianna, Oisín and Caoilte, crash through the time barrier and fast-forward some 200 years to join up with St Patrick and his followers as they travel on their mission around the land of Éireann. As the narrative unfolds, Patrick is distracted from his Christian duties as he listens to tales of times past when the Fianna were at the height of their powers under the leadership of Fionn.

THE COLLOQUY OF THE ANCIENTS
IN THE BOOK OF LISMORE

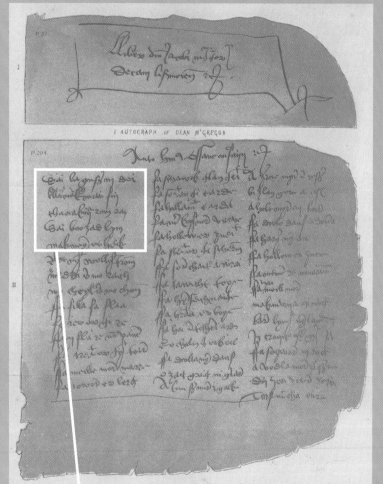

This is a facsimile page from the *Book of the Dean of Lismore*, which contains Scottish versions of Finian legends. It is a poem in praise of Fionn.

'It was yesterday week
I last saw Fionn
Never did I see
A braver man...'

THE 'COLLOQUY' TRACT must have been one of those preserved in the now-lost *Book of Monasterboise*, which was clearly used during the compiling of *Lismore* at the Franciscan Monastery of Timoleague, Co. Cork, around 1480. At folio 151 the Finian material begins with a short tract on the ten conditions for entering Fionn's warrior band, the Fianna. This is then followed by the unique tract variously described as the 'Discourse of the Ancients' or the 'Colloquy of the Elders of Ireland'. What it amounts to is a series of flashbacks to ancient heroic times occasioned by questions posed by St Patrick to long-surviving members of the Fianna about the meaning of the names of places to which they travel together. In each case Caoilte or Oisín tells a tale about the activities of the Fianna that brought about the naming of the place concerned. For example, Patrick asks, 'Why is the hill on which we stand called Fair Hill?' 'I will tell you the truth,' says Caoilte. 'It is from here that we went in our three battalions to fight the battle of Fair Shore or Ventry Strand.' He then goes on to tell the sad love story of Cael and Crede associated with this battle. Up to 200 tales are introduced in this way as the warriors make two circuits of Ireland in the company of Patrick.

A number of themes run throughout the narratives, principal of which is the sheer excellence of their leader Fionn. He and his band of warriors are presented as living in the privileged position of being of this world and yet very much in touch with the *sidh*, or spiritual realms of the Tuatha De Danann. Combining Otherworld magic with this-world heroics, the narrative is like our present-day fictions of *Harry Potter* and *The Lord of the Rings* rolled into one.

Like many of the late twelfth-century compositions, there is an effort in the 'Colloquy' to blend elements of the pagan world with the reformed Christian ethos of the time. The rather ingenious device of having heroes of old leapfrog over centuries of time to join up with St Patrick is an effective and intriguing one, which makes this tract, 'The Colloquy of the Ancients', one of the true gems found in the ancient books. As the oldest, most complete source document for the Finian or Ossianic Cycle, it gives the *dramatis personae*, the place settings and the storylines for many of the sagas later written about Fionn and his Fianna.

Across the hills and vales of Ireland this sprinkling of legend still clings to the places mentioned in the narrative and still enlivens the pride of place that is so much a part of how we view this land of ours.

There is no way of summarising the 'Colloquy'. It simply has to be read, and the best reading of it that I have found is that produced by Oxford Press in its *Tales of the Ancients of Ireland* (*Acallam na Senórach*).[5]

Conditions for entry to the Fianna from the Book of Lismore

To be accepted into Fionn's elite band, the candidate had to fulfil ten conditions:

1 He had to be a poet.
2 He had to fight off nine attacking warriors without being wounded, while restrained in a hole in the ground.
3 With just the distance of one tree as a head start, he must evade pursuers when running through one of the chief woods of Ireland.
4 Not a hair from his woven head must be found on a tree in the wood.
5 While running, his weapons must not tremble in his hands.
6 He should not break even a withered stick under foot.
7 He must be able to stoop under a branch as low as his knee.
8 He must leap a branch high as his ear.
9 He should be able to pluck out a thorn from his heel without breaking his stride.
10 His family should pledge not to sue his slayer in combat.

THE HISTORY OF THE
BOOK OF LISMORE

1177–1450

The book, as we now know it, begins with these lines: '*This is Patrick's Life; and let every one who shall read give a blessing for the souls of the couple for whom this book hath been written.*'[6] As indicated in a tract on folio 116, the 'couple' involved were Finghin MacCarthy Reagh, son of Gaelic Lord of Carbery Diarmait an Duma, and Caitilin, daughter of the Anglo-Irish Earl of Desmond. The *Book of Lismore* was thus compiled as a wedding present on the occasion of this union between a leader of the ancient Irish County Cork sept of MacCarthy and the daughter of the very much Norman-descended Earl of Desmond.

In the latter part of the tenth century the MacCarthys had wrested power in south Munster or 'Desmond' from the declining descendants of Brian Boru, the O'Briens. But they then had to contend with increasing pressure from the Anglo-Norman Fitzmorris/Fitzgerald family. From between 1177 and 1450, or so, hundreds of battles had been fought between these two family groups and thousands of their members had been killed. In the late fifteenth century, however, a truce of sorts was reached between them. By this time the Norman family Fitzgerald had become Earls of Desmond, while the MacCarthys still retained the ancient Gaelic title Kings of Desmond. Both groups were at this time allied in trying to stave off further attempts by London to impose ever tighter controls on all of Ireland.

Hence it was an alliance of no mean importance when in the final years of the 1400s Finghin MacCarthy (MacCarthaigh Riabhach) and Caitilin, daughter of Thomas, Earl of Desmond, were pledged to wed. The *Book of Lismore* was created as part of the celebration. This fact is noted in a number of introductory poems in the book and the names Caitilin and Finghin appear on Folio 116.

It is not surprising that the 'Colloquy of the Ancients' should be included in the contents, since both the marriage and the tract itself had to do with the joining of two cultures — the Norman and old Gaelic on the one hand, the Christian and ancient Druidic on the other.

1480

It is generally accepted that the *Book of Lismore* was compiled at the Franciscan Monastery at Timoleague, Co. Cork, which, since its foundation around 1465, had been solidly supported by the MacCarthy kings. Its actual writing in the library there was probably completed around 1480 in time for the wedding.

—— 1629 ——

The next we know of the book is almost 150 years later when one of the Four Masters, Micheal O'Clery, used it to copy some Lives of the Saints during a visit to Timoleague in 1629.

—— 1641–1642 ——

Soon afterwards, during the Irish uprising of 1641, the turbulent story of the book begins. By that time it was housed at the MacCarthy stronghold of Kilbrittain Castle. In 1642 this was attacked by the British forces, headed by a man who was known as 'the Terror of Munster', the Governor of Bandon, Lord Kinalmeaky. He was son to Lord Justice of the English administration in Ireland, Richard Boyle, Earl of Cork, whose seat was at Lismore Castle.

Having taken Kilbrittain, Kinalmeaky wrote a letter to his father on June 25, 1642 in which he makes mention of having confiscated an ancient book from the castle, which he was sending on as a gift. He himself was killed just three months later in an attack on Liscarroll. But his confiscated gift to his father appears to have been our *Book of Lismore* and this explains how it got from the MacCarthy Castle to the place on the Blackwater that gave it its present name.

On this map of Munster (1616), the territories of the Earl of Desmond and the McCarthy's are marked out.

—— 1643 ——

Just one year later, in 1643, Lismore Castle was itself attacked by Confederate Irish forces under Lord Muskerry and it may well have been at this point that the book was sealed up in a passage within the castle for safe-keeping.

—— 1814–1820 ——

It was not re-discovered until 1814 when restoration work on the interior of the building was undertaken by the then owner, the Duke of Devonshire.

The ruins of Timoleague Abbey where the *Book of Lismore* was compiled. The library would appear to have been in the upper floor of the builing on the right.

A print of Lismore Castle dating from about the time when the great *Book of Lismore* lay buried and gnawed by rats behind a bricked-up wall.

There is a problem with this theory, however, since a date of 1745 is written onto folio 55 by someone who was apparently reading the story of Charlemagne's campaign against the Saracens, which was written on that page, and trying to determine the time lapsed between the date of Mohammed's death and their own time. So we have to say that the book was sealed up within the walls of Lismore Castle either from 1643 when the castle was attacked or from 1745 when this note was made. This remains a mystery but either way it stayed hidden until a workman knocked a piece of wall in 1814, found there a secret passage and in it a box containing both the *Book of Lismore* and a beautiful gold-plated crosier that had been made for the Abbot of Lismore around 1100.

While incarcerated within the wall, the *Book of Lismore* became, on more than one occasion, the dinner for rats and mice. Since it had been rolled up into a bundle, the outer leaves at the back suffered most both from the gnawing rodents and from the damp which penetrated the box.

But this was only the beginning of the book's troubles. Because of its loose, unbound state, a number of its leaves were immediately pillaged at the time of the find and never recovered. During the following year the book was put into the 'safe-keeping' of the Duke of Devonshire's agent Colonel Curry. For some unknown reason Curry then loaned the manuscript to a rather untrustworthy Corkman named Dennis O'Flynn, who pretended to be using it for research but in fact appeared bent on making money out of it.

Doing more damage than the rats had ever done, O'Flynn first set about trying to enhance the book's looks by inserting capitals in spaces left by the original scribes. These are of the most hideous design and are a caricature of the professional illuminations that were no doubt intended but never inserted.

In addition to the 'capitals', O'Flynn used a heavy, dead black ink to scribble in the book and touch up some faded sections throughout. The next crime against the book was the application of some chemical

Chatsworth House in England, where the *Book of Lismore* is now preserved in the extensive library of the Earl of Devonshire.

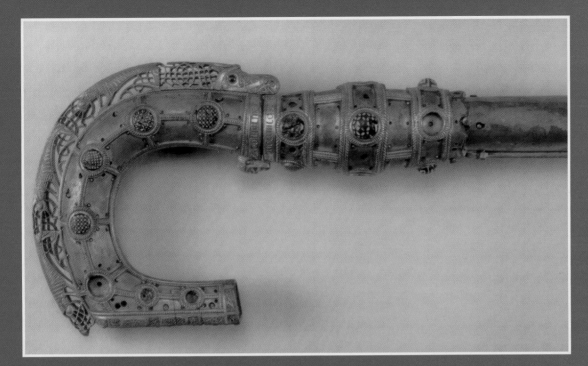

The eleventh-century crosier found with the *Book of Lismore* in 1814 during restoration work at Lismore Castle.

that was intended to increase legibility but which in fact just blackened a number of pages, thus making them all but unreadable.

Exactly what O'Flynn was up to is not all that clear, but Eugene O'Curry, who made an exhaustive study of the problem, came to the conclusion that the Corkman first of all made copies of the book for sale. Then, before returning it to Lismore sometime prior to 1820, he separated off key sections, 66 folios in all, whose absence from the volume would enhance the value of copies he had made.

—— 1839–1861 ——

To disguise O'Flynn's confiscation, when returning the remaining 131 folios to Lismore Castle, he bound them in thick boards. It was in fact a further 20 years before the theft of pages was discovered by Eugene O'Curry when he was commissioned by the Royal Irish Academy to make a facsimile of *Lismore* in 1839. He thus records his horror when he found that 'not only whole staves had been pilfered but particular subjects had been mutilated so as to leave the part returned to Lismore almost valueless without the abstracted parts, the offending parties having first, of course, copied all or the most part of the mutilated pieces'.[7]

So incensed was O'Curry by what he had found out, he began what proved to be a 15-year search for the missing folios. Like a good detective, he pieced together the evidence so that by 1853 he was in a position to ask a friend of his in Cork to 'endeavour to ascertain in whose hands it was, what might be the nature of the contents, whether it would be sold and at what price'.[8]

Well, in fact there was a price on the missing pages — of £50 — and this O'Curry and some friends at the Royal Irish Academy were willing to pay. However, at the last moment negotiations on the transfer broke down and there was further delay. But the investigation he had initiated was not in vain, for in a brief note added to the Index of his *Lectures*, O'Curry states: 'The Cork part of it has been restored to the original *Book of Lismore* since delivery of these Lectures.' And that would have to have been sometime between July 10, 1856 and the date of publication in 1861.

With some 46 folios at the beginning still missing and a few from the end of the 'Colloquy of the Ancients', it is estimated that the book still lacks in the region of 50 of its original leaves. All remaining 197 have been removed from Lismore Castle to the Duke of Devonshire's English estate at Chatsworth House in Derbyshire, where it is part of a vast library that has recently been valued at about £90m.

—— 1940s ——

The *Book of Lismore* was loaned to the Irish Manuscripts Commission in the late 1940s and this resulted in a photographic collotype facsimile being created at the British Museum. This was published in 1950 by the Irish Stationery Office with an introduction and notes by R.A.S. Macalister. In this photographic copy, evidence of the destruction done to the book can clearly be seen, yet the vast majority of pages are still quite legible.

Several sections of the book have been translated and published. Most notably Standish O'Grady included a good English version of the 'Colloquy' in his 1892 *Silva Gadelica*. More recently, in 1999, Oxford

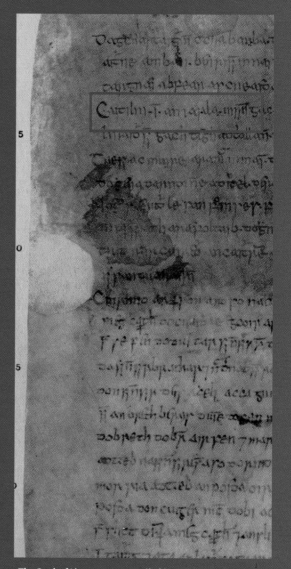

The *Book of Lismore* was compiled in 1480 as a wedding present for Finghin MacCarthy Reagh and Caitilin, daughter of the Earl of Desmond. Caitlin's name appears on this rather faded page (p.116 of the photographic facsimile of the text).

University Press produced the superb new translation by University of Toronto academics Ann Dooley and Harry Roe under the title *Tales of the Elders of Ireland*.

The uniquely atmospheric Lives of Irish Saints, which take up the first 50 pages or so of *Lismore,* have been in print since 1890 through a masterful piece of work by Whitley Stokes.

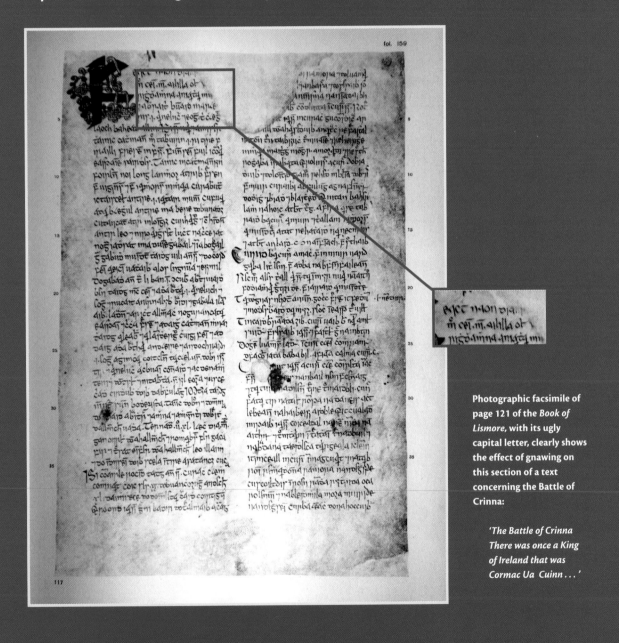

Photographic facsimile of page 121 of the *Book of Lismore*, with its ugly capital letter, clearly shows the effect of gnawing on this section of a text concerning the Battle of Crinna:

'The Battle of Crinna
There was once a King
of Ireland that was
Cormac Ua Cuinn...'

CONTENTS OF THE BOOK OF LISMORE

SINCE THE OCCASION for the creation of the book was the bringing together of two very differing traditions — Finghin MacCarthy Reagh, son of Gaelic Lord of Carbery Diarmait an Duma, and Caitilin, daughter of the Anglo-Irish Earl of Desmond — it is understandable that a very varied selection of material would have been included. In addition to the Fionn Mac Cumhaill material there are regal tracts, Lives of the Saints, pious poems, biblical tales and other imported tracts that must have been popular with the learned classes in Ireland of the time.

It is fascinating to find sprinkled throughout the various stories and episodes recorded phrases and anecdotes that have become utterly familiar to us without us ever knowing where their early version is to be found. For example, at the very beginning of the book, in a homily on the life of St Patrick, we find a rather humorous piece of dialogue between the saint and a new convert, Oengus: '*Now when Patrick was blessing the head of Oengus, the spike of the crosier went through his foot. So, after the end of the benediction, when Patrick saw the wound he said, 'Why did you not tell me?' Said Oengus, 'I thought it was a rite of the faith.'* That story has been used many times down the ages in reference to Ireland's particular kind of devotion to the faith.[9]

Then in the Life of Brigit we find the joining of her Christian persona with her alter ego, the goddess Brigit of the ancient Druidic world, through Maithgin the wizard who prophesies the saint's greatness while she was still in the womb of a bondsmaid: '*The bondsmaid will bring forth a daughter conspicuous, radiant, who will shine like the sun among the stars of heaven.*'[10]

Here too we find the story of how St Ciaran's cow Odhar followed him from home to Clonard where she helped feed the whole community. Of her fame after that the book has this to say: '*Now the Dune's hide is in Clonmacnoise, and what soul so ever separates from its body on that*

Image of St Brigit, whose life was recorded in the *Book of Lismore* along with many other Irish saints.

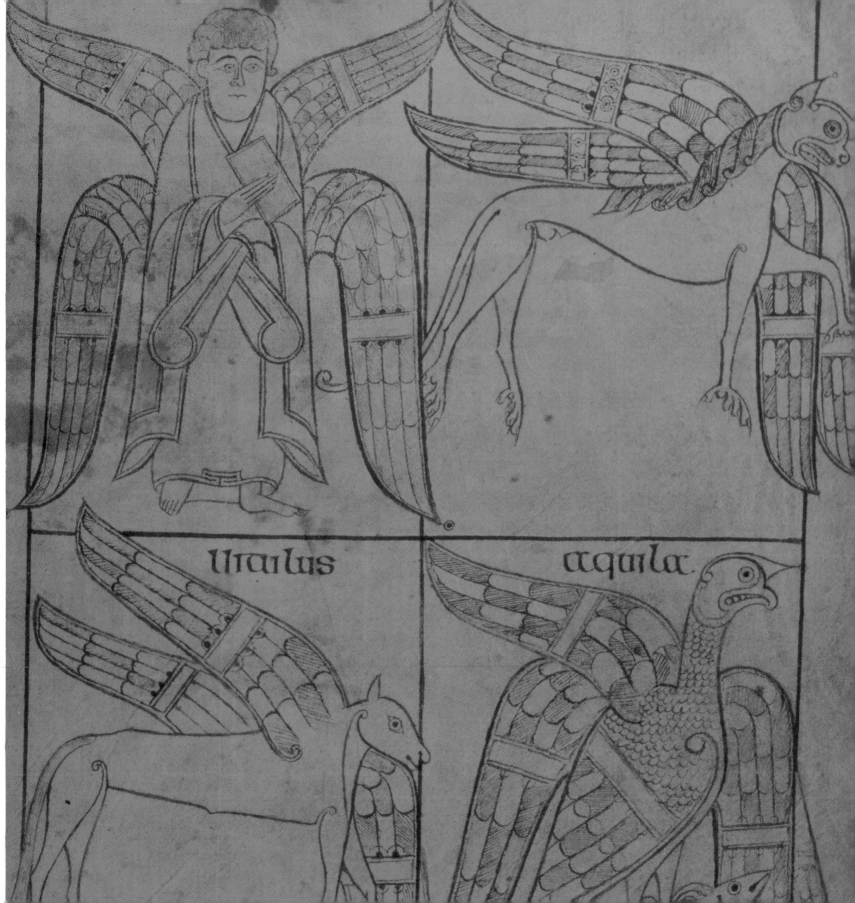

uitulus

aquila

HISTORY OF
LEBOR NA HUIDRE

— AD807 —

The book was penned by the learned scribe of Armagh, Ferdomnach, along with two assistants, around the year AD807.

— AD845 —

After Ferdomnach's death in AD845, the book was given the name *Canon of St Patrick*. As a consequence, the real author's name was pushed into the background and then eventually erased altogether. The *Canon of St Patrick* joined the saint's staff and bell as one of the three sacred objects connected with Ireland's Apostle, which had to be in the possession of anyone claiming to be his successor in the Primal Archbishopric of Armagh.

— 1005 —

In 1005, during his circuit of Ireland, High King Brian Boru visited Armagh where he recognised the primacy of the Church there over other churches in Ireland and confirmed its right to levy tribute on the other ecclesiastical foundations around the country. Among the objects on display during the course of his visit was the *Canon of St Patrick*. His soul friend Mael Suthain, who accompanied him, recorded the occasion in the sacred book on the reverse side of folio 16 with the following words:

'When going to heaven, St Patrick decreed that the entire fruit of his labours, and baptisms and of the causes of alms should be rendered to the apostolic city which in the Scotish tongue is called Ardmacha. Thus I have found it to be in the books of the Scots. I Mael Suthain write this in the presence of Brian, Emperor of the Scots [Irish] and what I have written he has determined on behalf of all the kings of Cashel.'[2]

Eugene O'Curry's very readable facsimile of the Brian Boru inscription in the *Book of Armagh*.

In this way Brian, then at the very height of his powers as a true high king of all Ireland, was giving his approval to the claims that Armagh had primacy at the head of the Irish Church and was thus entitled to monies being given to it.

—— 1144 ——

In 1144, when the great reformer of the Irish Church, St Malachy, was bidding to become Archbishop of Armagh, the book came into play once more. His rival Niall, the last of the Ui Sinaich family to control the Primal See, fled with the book and St Patrick's staff and bell. As a result, he temporarily won popular support for his claim to the Primacy. Later Malachy gained the upper hand and the sacred objects were returned to Armagh.

—— 1681 ——

It was probably after the Malachy/Niall episode that the hereditary Keeper or *Maor na Canoine* was given greater powers to look after the book. This became a lucrative hereditary post passed on within the one family up until 1681. Hence the derivation of the name MacMoyer or *Mac Maor*. This was no small honour since along with the title went estates of eight townlands in the Barony of Upper Fews, Co. Armagh. These comprised over 7,000 acres that had an estimated annual rental income of £3,000. So the MacMoyers had much to gain from the reverence in which the book was held. It may well have been them that attempted to ensure the continuance of this state of affairs by erasing the true author's name. Incidentally the *Canon of St Patrick* was also much in demand for the registering of oaths, so much so that the page on which hands were placed in this act of swearing is severely faded.

An ancient bell usually associated with St Patrick. Possession of the bell, along with St Patrick's staff and the *Book of Armagh*, were considered to give the right to hold the Archbishopric of Armagh.

The MacMoyers held on to the book, but during the Plantation of Ulster they lost all their lands. By the time the notorious Florence MacMoyer took on the title (possibly around 1662), his possessions were reduced to a small holding on the ancestral lands which he now had to rent from the new owners, the Fairfaxs. As noted by Alice Curtayne in her book *The Trial of Oliver Plunkett*, this man was weighed down with bitterness during the time he gave his false evidence at the Archbishop of Armagh's trial in 1681. She also notes that as a reward for his damning testimony, he was promised 'an estate as good as ever his grandfather had'.[3] Having been condemned to die at Tyburn, Oliver Plunkett made a speech from the dock in which he referred to his accusers as 'merciless perjurers'.[4]

It is an ultimate irony that in order to make his way to London for the trial in 1681, Florence pawned for the measly sum of £5 the sacred book that had earned his forefathers those same estates. Sadly, the book carries the autograph of this pathetic individual on the back of its folio 104: '*Liber Florentium Muire — Junio 29, 1662*'. MacMoyer neither recovered his patrimony nor the great book, and until his death in 1713 he lived out his life in 'abject poverty and detestation'.[5]

—— **1707** ——

Some short time after becoming a pawn, the *Book of Armagh* must have been put on the public market. In 1707 it was mentioned in antiquarian Edward Lhuyd's *Catalogue of Irish Manuscripts* as being the property of an Arthur Brownlaw of Lurgan, Co. Armagh. Quoting a letter he had received from the then owner, Lhuyd referred to it not as *Canoin Padraig* but as *Leabar Arda Macha, Book of Armagh* — the first record we have of it being so called — and the name has stuck ever since.

It was the possession of the Brownlaw family for the next century and a half, and during most of that time it remained in total obscurity.

St Oliver Plunkett, whose sentence to death in 1681 was partly due to the money derived by one of his accusers through pawning the *Book of Armagh* for £5.

—— **1846-1847** ——

The fifth-generation descendant, Reverend Francis Brownlaw, then introduced it into the academic world. In 1846 he reached agreement with the Royal Irish Academy to deposit it in the Academy's museum so that it could be studied there. The agreement read that it was deposited 'with the understanding that the Academy will take the same care of the book as they do of the best articles in their Museum; and that the Academy will at any time return the said book to the said Rev. Francis Brownlaw or his heirs or representatives on his or their demand, and without any delay, charge or hindrance whatever'.[6]

Armagh, Ireland's Primal Ecclesiastical See, dating back to the time of St Patrick.

When Francis Brownlaw died in 1847, his son and heir allowed the book to remain at the Academy, and it was during this time that Charles Graves was able to conduct his test to discover its true authorship by Ferdomnach.

—— 1853 ——

The book was featured in the great Dublin Exhibition run by the RDS at Leinster House Lawn in 1853. But surprisingly, at the end of its descriptive card on the display case were appended the words 'To Be Sold'. Sold it was within a short time for £300 to manuscript expert Dr William Reeves. He retained it only long enough to publish a very valuable study on it. Then, for the same price he paid for it, Reeves sold it on to the Protestant Archbishop of Armagh, Lord John George Beresford. The Archbishop also happened to be Chancellor of Trinity College, Dublin, at the time and upon receipt of the precious book he immediately deposited it in the Library of Trinity, where to this day it is on permanent display side by side with the magnificent *Book of Kells*.

Its *cumdach* or shrine had long since been separated from it when it came to Trinity, but with it then was a strong leather satchel with Celtic design, which, while too large for the diminutive book itself, might well have been the right size for its now-lost former shrine.

The leather cover of the *Book of Armagh*, which at one time may also have covered the book's shrine. This drawing was made by George Petrie for his book on Irish round towers.

—— 1913 ——

Taking up work begun by Dr Reeves, Dr John Gwynn of Trinity College completed a beautiful, word-for-word printed transcript of the book in 1913 for the Royal Irish Academy, of which 400 copies were produced. It includes an introduction of almost 300 pages on every aspect of the text.

CONTENTS OF THE BOOK OF ARMAGH

SOME HAVE SAID THAT compared with its companions in Trinity like the *Book of Kells* and the *Book of Durrow*, *Armagh* appears plain and dull. But that observation is only colour deep, for inside this volume is some of the oldest and richest material available on the early Irish Church. Its neatly written double column pages bring us deep into the heart of what it was like for a Christian man to enter Ireland in the fifth century with the intention of confronting the old ways of the Druids and preaching a whole new way of life to the people here. Be his name Patrick or whoever; be he as successful in his mission as the legends within this book tell us he was, there can be no mistaking the human dread he felt as he approached the 'stronghold of Irish royalty and heathenism' at Tara. This story is laid out here in great detail; so too is the soul-searching of this missionary man in his 'Confession'. And included as well is the most complete copy we have of the main tool of this daring apostle's trade, the Vulgate New Testament of the new dispensation that he preached.

As the *Book of Armagh* now stands, it has 215 of its original vellum leaves. The very first leaf is missing and so are four others in the middle of St Matthew's Gospel. One page, which easily opens between two of the Gospels, appears to have been the one constantly used for the taking of oaths, and hence, because of the thousands of hands laid upon it, it is severely faded. Other than that, this volume is intact and as legible today as when Ferdomnach wrote it almost 1200 years ago.

It has three main sections — the material relating to St Patrick, the New Testament and a Life of St Martin of Tours. It is thought that the scribe Ferdomnach planned that all three sections were to stand on their own: 1) The story of Patrick, which was undertaken as an argument for the Primacy of the scribe's home place of Armagh in the life of the Irish Church in his time; 2) the Gospels and Epistles that could be carried for reading in local churches; and 3) the Life of St Martin of Tours, who was a much-venerated saint and a relative of St Patrick, with whom Patrick was reputed to have studied prior to his Irish mission.

Now it is clearly a fact that of all those pages, the ones that have down the centuries had the greatest impact are those relating to St Patrick. First there is his life story as written in the late seventh century by Muirchu Maccu Machtheni, who worked from sources in Leinster and Ulster to create a very vivid picture of the saint.

Then there are the memoirs of Patrick by Tirechan, followed by a section called the *Liber Angeli*, attributed to Patrick himself, about the rights of the Church of Armagh, and finally the Confession. The latter is Patrick's own defence of his mission here and is thought to have been copied from his own autograph by Ferdomnach. So herein lie the oldest versions we have of the stories, legends and devotions associated with St Patrick which have so informed our thinking about this man and the time in which he lived. A good deal of how we view ourselves and how others view us from around the world has grown out of the words put down on these pages back in AD807.

There were other ancient Lives of St Patrick written, and a number of these were later collated into what is called 'The Tripartite Life'. This is a compilation in three main parts of sermons about Patrick that were written down in Gaelic and Latin around AD900. The oldest copy we have of 'The Tripartite Life' dates from the time of the Four Masters in the seventeenth century. So here, in the first 24 folia of the *Book of Armagh*, we have the oldest, most basic material on St Patrick.

For the Irish Christians of the ninth century, when this book was written, Patrick was their Christ — a wonder-worker of immense power— and as far as they were concerned this was his own sacred testament.

The note on folio 24v, which gave rise to the belief that St Patrick himself was author of the Book of Armagh:

'Thus far the book which Patrick wrote with his own hand; the 17th day of March Patrick went to heaven.'

MUIRCHU'S LIFE OF PATRICK

APPROPRIATELY ENOUGH, the *Book of Armagh* begins with the oldest and most respected Life of St Patrick. It was written by Muirchu sometime in the late seventh century under the direction of

Aedh, who was Bishop of Sletty in County Laois. Covering both sides of the first eight folia, it also has a preface that is misplaced later on in the book at folio 20. The Life is made up of two main sections. First there is a very descriptive narrative about St Patrick's young years as a slave shepherd boy, his escape, education and ordination on the Continent and his return to Ireland. This section ends with Patrick's triumph at Tara. The second section presents glimpses of his later missionary travels throughout Ireland and includes a description of 16 major miracles.

It is interesting that both the author Muirchu and the promoter Aedh were said to have attended the Synod at Tara in AD697 when the powerful leader of the Irish Church, Adamnan, promulgated his reform document *Lex Innocentium*. It may well have been as a result of this meeting at the place so identified with the national Apostle that the plan to write a Life of St Patrick gained impetus.

It is also interesting that it was Aedh of Sletty who promoted the idea, since he was successor to St Fiacc, who was said to have been one of those converted by Patrick during his dramatic visit to Tara in AD433. Fiacc went on to be the first Bishop of Sletty, and it could be that it was his firsthand knowledge of events at Tara, carefully preserved at Sletty, that Aedh was passing on to Muirchu some 264 years later. Anyway, the confrontation between Patrick, High King Laoghaire and the Druids at Tara is the high point of this narrative account of the saint's life.

But Muirchu had more than this one Sletty source at his disposal during his writing of the biography. His opening episodes about Patrick's early life are clearly drawn directly from the saint's own *Confession*. It is thought that he was either using the original autograph of Patrick or else an early copy of it. His clarity in describing the topography of the northeast would indicate that he also used sources from places like St Patrick's dying spot, Saul, near Downpatrick.

All of this combined to create a uniquely clear, though miracle-driven, picture of St Patrick's existence in mid-fifth-century Ireland. The result is basic material that has informed the picture we have of St Patrick — a young man captured and brought to pagan Ireland; in his

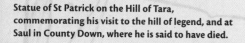

Statue of St Patrick on the Hill of Tara, commemorating his visit to the hill of legend, and at Saul in County Down, where he is said to have died.

solitude finding God; dramatically escaping; receiving his mission to return with a new faith to this island and then confronting the old religion in its most powerful centres.

THE MEMOIR OF TIRECHAN

IN CONTRAST TO THE fairly flowing narrative of Muirchu, *The Memoir of Tirechan*, written somewhat earlier in AD670, is really a list of episodes in St Patrick's life designed to emphasise the Primacy of Armagh in governing the various parts of the Church in Ireland. The emphasis is on the churches established by the Apostle himself.

Tirechan hailed from Tirawley in County Mayo but was a disciple of the Bishop of Ardbraccan near Navan, St Ultan, who supplied him with much of the material relating to Tara and to Meath. In addition to serving the political purpose for which it was presumably written, his memoir is also responsible for helping to create a whole new Christian

The holy well at Ardbraccan, near Navan, Co. Meath, named after St Ultan, who commissioned his disciple Tirechan to write his memoir of St Patrick.

topography of Ireland. While retaining many of the old pre-Patrician place names, he adds a new layer of identity based on saints' names and the churches they established, which has lasted right down to our present day. One could call this a Christian *Dindshenchas* superimposed upon the ancient *Dindshenchas* or oral legend that preceded the arrival of the new religion. Down the ages these two topographies have existed side by side — for example, places with *rath* in their name next to places beginning with *cill*. The word *rath*, as in Rathmore, for example, would have had an association with an ancient ringfort in the area, while the word *Cill*, anglicised to Kil, as in Kilronan, had reference to a particular saint's foundation or church.

The Memoir of Tirechan begins in Meath and includes a very vivid but somewhat less fantastic description than Muirchu's of the 'confrontation' at Tara. It then proceeds to follow Patrick as he preaches, converts, ordains disciples and establishes churches along a circuit that brings him to Longford, Roscommon, across the Shannon to Mayo, then north to Donegal, across to Antrim, down into Meath once more and from there south through Leinster and into Munster at the royal site of Cashel. Along the way he records the well-known stories of Patrick's 40-day sojourn on Croagh Patrick and the conversion of King Laoghaire's two daughters, Eithne and Fedelemidh, at the sacred well near the Druid college of Cruachan.

Tirechan makes it appear that this was one continuous circuit of Ireland by the saint, but it is more probable that it is a compilation of many trips. It may well be that the author followed Patrick's footsteps in order to gain local knowledge of events.

Just as with Muirchu, Tirechan's Memoir is written in two parts — the first brings Patrick as far as the Shannon and the second ends at Cashel. Somewhat like footnotes, added by Ferdomnach himself, there is discussion about the age of St Patrick and the date of his mission. Scholars still argue over these same questions, but it is now generally agreed that the saint came to Ireland in AD432 and that he died thirty years later in AD462. At least some of what he accomplished during the intervening years is laid down here by Tirechan, who has established connections between Patrick and many, many areas around the country that are still familiarly referred to today, like Croagh Patrick in County Mayo, St Patrick's Purgatory in Donegal, St Patrick's Rock in Cashel or Slieve Patrick near his burial place in County Down.

THE LIBER ANGELI

IT IS NOW GENERALLY agreed that the overall purpose of Tirechan's Memoir and the reason for its inclusion in this book was to strengthen Armagh's claim to supremacy over the churches of Ireland. To further make that point, Ferdomnach also added on to Tirechan an eighth-century tract called *Liber Angeli*, which, on folia 20 and 21, purports to record a colloquy between St Patrick and an angel in which the rights of the Primal See were laid out. This is indeed serious stuff involving not only authority in the spiritual world but in temporal financial matters as well. '*Every church in the whole Island of the Scots is by God's donation in the special society of Patrick and the Heir of the See of Armagh.*'[6] Nothing could be plainer than that — Armagh was in control.

But the very last note in this section indicates that there could be exceptions to this overall power of Armagh. This is in the case of St Brigid of Kildare, who is described as being the object of 'loving friendship' on the part of St Patrick. Her church is therefore accorded certain exemptions from the overall precepts governing other establishments in the rest of Leinster and beyond.

Thus ends the section of the book in which a narrator has been telling us of Patrick, his actions, his travels and his thoughts. Most of it was first written down between 200 and 250 years after the saint's death. In other words, it is as if someone in our own time were now trying to write the story of George Washington or the exploits of Daniel O'Connell or Wolfe Tone. Just as with these heroes from history, legend sometimes overshadows fact and the politics of the time of writing has a bearing on the approach taken. But in the next section of the *Book of Armagh*, we come to what is seen as the unadulterated outpourings from the heart of St Patrick himself in his own *Confession*.

I have made known with simplicity.... For what reason I have preached and do now preach, to strengthen and confirm your faith Would that you too may follow greater examples and do better things. This would be my glory, for a wise child is a father's glory

A translation of the beginning of St Patrick's *Confession* from the *Book of Armagh*.

THE CONFESSION OF ST PATRICK

Here we have a cry from the spiritual heart of a man at the dawn of Christianity in Ireland. Putting himself in danger of his life, he rejects the old ways while at the same time stoutly defending the new. *'The sun rises daily for our sakes,'* he says, *'but all those who worship it perish while those who believe in the true Christ will not perish.'* Brave stuff this, in the face of a culture that had devotion to the earth mother goddesses and the power of the sun at the centre of its beliefs.

This *Confession* is the testimony of a man with the right approach to the Irish scene — no proud airs from him but rather a declaration of his own ignorance and sinfulness. He sees his weakness being raised up by the power of one single God that would do the same for the Irish with whom he came to share the new faith.

He declares that he was called by 'The Voice of the Irish' and, though an 'uneducated man', he accepted the commission to be a messenger. And on this basis he defends himself against some of his contemporary detractors, who appear to have questioned his right to be a missionary and a bishop in the land of the Gael.

The *Confession* is composed of some 60 sayings that cover just two and a half folia. It is introduced after the two Lives and the *Liber Angeli* on folio 22 with no great fanfare, not even a decorated initial, but in fact it is the beating heart of this book and puts us in touch with what the volume is really all about — St Patrick himself. He wrote it, and while this is a copy and not his original autograph, it does spring out at us as his own words delivered out of that twilight time when he brought his new message to the very people who had previously enslaved him.

In it he describes times when he danced with death: *'and on that day they most eagerly desired to kill me'*. And he concludes *'Receive this writing which Patrick the sinner composed in Ireland. It is the gift of God and this is my Confession before I die.'* After these words on the reverse of folio 24, Ferdomnach inserted this note: *'Huc usque volumen quod Patricius manu conscripsit sua; septima decima Martii die translatus est Patricius ad caelos'* (*'Thus far the book which Patrick wrote with his own hand; on the 17th day of March Patrick went to heaven'*).

There has been a great deal of learned discussion about just what source Patrick used in the many scriptural quotes he included in his *Confession* — Old Latin or St Jerome's Vulgate. If Old Latin, this gels nicely with his authorship, since it was still widely used in Patrick's time. If Jerome's Vulgate, then it presents problems as to how the saint would have acquired a copy of this version at such an early date, since Jerome did not complete his work until around AD387 and it did not become generally used in the Church at large until the seventh century. Experts now appear agreed that most of the quotes are indeed from the Old Latin version and any that appear to lean towards Jerome are put down to the scribe writing a phrase in the version most familiar to him at his time of copying.

Beside the *Armagh*, at least five other versions of the *Confession* exist — all dating from the eleventh or twelfth centuries. In 1905 Dr Newport White of Trinity College constructed one critical edition out of all six and confirmed that the *Armagh* text is quite incomplete.[7] While retaining the energy of the saint, Ferdomnach's version is missing about one third of the original. Why this should be so is difficult to tell. The best and most sensible explanation is that there were pages either missing or illegible in the

The distinctive four Gospel symbols of the *Book of Armagh*.

exemplar used by the Armagh scribe. Ferdomnach was working with a very early version, possibly even the original autograph of Patrick. After what could have been some 300 years of revered use, it is not surprising that parts of the *Confession* could have been lost. If Ferdomnach was using a version very close to the original, then this would explain his statement at its conclusion: '*Thus far the book which Patrick wrote with his own hand*'. Other copies of this document had been made and some of them included a number of accretions. This, along with the loss of pages, would explain the difference in length between the *Armagh* version and others edited by Dr White.

THE NEW TESTAMENT

Filling over 100 of the folia that follow the *Confession* is *Armagh*'s copy of the New Testament. This is revered as being the oldest complete Irish copy of St Jerome's Vulgate and brings us into contact with the Gospels and Epistles as read in the Early Irish Church. It is a very workmanlike copy, which is quite plain in contrast to the less complete but more ornate versions in the *Book of Kells* or the *Book of Durrow*. However, at the beginning of each Gospel and at the start of the various epistles, etc., there are some very interesting decorative capitals.

There are also some black and white drawings of the Gospel symbols. First there is the Gospel of Matthew, and directly preceding it there are a number of introductory tracts like the Letter of Eusebius to Pope Gregory and a list of the headings in the whole New Testament. The Gospel of Mark is next followed by Luke and then John. The latter has the most elaborate capital and symbol of all.

LIFE OF ST MARTIN OF TOURS

The *Book of Armagh* ends with the Life of St Martin of Tours. Why this should be so is not easy to tell. This section of the book, which is more highly decorated than the rest, may have at one time existed as a separate volume that was only later added in. Its main function would appear to be that of bolstering the belief that St Patrick did visit with St Martin after escaping from Ireland. This in turn would back up the belief that St Patrick lived to be 120 years old and did not die until AD492. This is not now accepted by historians and hence the place of St Martin in his life has been somewhat downgraded. Yet arguments for a close association between the two saints put forward by people like William Bullen Morris in his 1891 publication *Ireland and St Patrick* still make interesting and fairly convincing reading.[8]

But Patrick living until 120? — no! We will have to put that down to legend. Indeed, there is much more that is legend in this fascinating book. But for generations it provided the accepted wisdom about St Patrick and the early years of Ireland's dramatic change from the world of Druidism to that of Christianity. Just how that change prospered under Columcille is the subject of our next chapter.

The ornate cover of what is usually known as St Patrick's Bell.

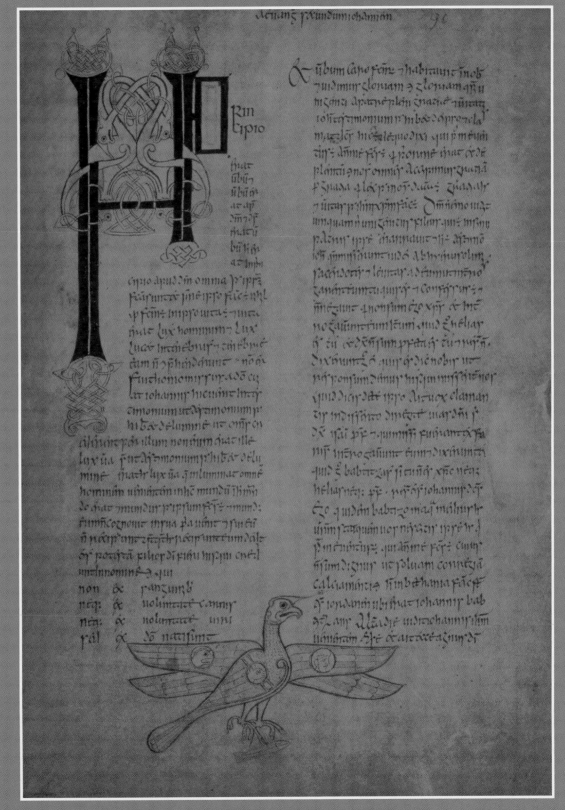

A more flamboyant page for the start of St John's Gospel in the *Book of Armagh.*

CHAPTER VI

Ireland's Oldest Book

The CATHACH
(*c.*AD600)

CREATED AS A BEAUTIFUL CHOIR BOOK OF THE PSALMS, IT DATES BACK SO NEAR TO THE TIME OF COLUMCILLE THAT IT IS FOREVER ASSOCIATED WITH HIS LEGENDS.

Opposite: Psalm 56 from the *Cathach*.

in placeum conando in iam me uiteraum

iur

Iserere mei ds miserere mei
quoniam in te confidit anima mea
& in umbra alarum tuarum
bo donec transeat iniquitas

Clamabo ad dm altissimum dm qui benefecit mihi
misit de caelo & liberauit me
dedit in obprobrium conculcantes me
misit ds misericordiam suam & ueritatem suam
Eripuit animam meam de medio catulorum leonum
dormiui conturbatus
filii hominum dentes eorum arma & sagittae

ts Irish name is *An Cathach*, 'The Battler', because of its use as a talisman of war by the O'Donnells of Donegal. It is the oldest extant Irish book and the world's second most ancient copy of the Psalms.

In legend, it is attributed to St Columcille himself, whose copying of a book of psalms sparked a deadly conflict between the northern and southern O'Neill kings in early medieval Ireland. However, there is no proof that this is the same book. But historians will admit that it could date back to very near Columcille's time in the late sixth century.

In short, it is a beautiful vellum volume that is wrapped in myth, mystery and the aura of the very beginnings of monasticism on these islands. Just 58 brave leaves have survived, which bring us back to a time when, in a land where writing had been taboo, suddenly the book was *all*, as holy men craved them and battles were fought over them.

One of the most distinctive capital letters from the *Cathach* – the *Qui Habitat*.

The beautiful shrine for the *Cathach*, commissioned by the O'Donnells of Donegal, who used the book as a battle talisman.

IRELAND AND THE WRITTEN WORD

IT IS GENERALLY AGREED that writing, as we understand it, did not come to Ireland until the arrival of Christianity in the fifth century. Prior to that time, intellectual life in the country was largely controlled by the Druidic and bardic orders within what was a totally oral tradition. It certainly was not in the Druids' or bards' best interests to promote the art of writing, since their position in society was dependent on their maintaining a certain monopoly over the sacred texts, sagas and ranns, which, through long years of study, they committed to memory.

The accepted wisdom on this matter is rooted in Julius Caesar's declaration about the Celts of Gaul: '*Neque fas esse existimant ea litteris mandare*' ('They consider it improper to commit their studies to writing').[1] No Celtic script has come down to us from the pre-Christian era to contradict that statement.

It is possible that the form of writing known as ogham was in limited use prior to the coming of Patrick. Named after the Tuatha De Danann god Ogma, who featured in the legend of the second battle of Magh Tuired, it is composed of some 20 letters written by way of differing uses of up to five parallel strokes. A good description of it was given in the *Book of Ballymote*. The great twentieth-century scholar R.A.S. Macalister copied hundreds of examples of it from around Ireland and Britain. He argued that it was originally a manual-signal alphabet used within 'Druidic freemasonry' as their secret stock-in-trade for the transmission of cryptic messages. He felt that by using five fingers in differing positions they could spell out the whole alphabet. He also argued that it was only in later times within the early Christian era that it took written form in parallel strokes chiselled onto standing stones.[2]

It is a fact that this form of script is totally impractical for any lengthy writings, and the examples we have of it are mostly brief memorials in burial places. Other than this, we have no examples of writing that could be attributed to the pre-Christian era.

From early Christian times, we have one very old Latin fragment of St Matthew's Gospel called the *Domhnach Airgid*, which historians date to the fifth or early sixth century and which could pre-date the *Cathach*, but 'The Battler' still holds the distinction of being the oldest Irish writing that can be termed a book.

Ireland's earliest native form of writing, ogham, which may have preceded the Latin script that came to our island in the fifth century with the arrival of Christianity. This example is from Dunloe, Co. Kerry.

The Domhnach Airgid

NAMED AFTER THE SHRINE (the 'Silver Church') in which it was found at Clones in County Monaghan, this small fragment of St Matthew's Gospel has become associated with the story of St Patrick's presentation of a gospel book to St Macartan at the time of his appointment to the See of Clogher. The older part of the shrine belongs to the eighth century, but the Gospel fragment itself is a good deal older than that. Some date it to the late fifth or early sixth century.

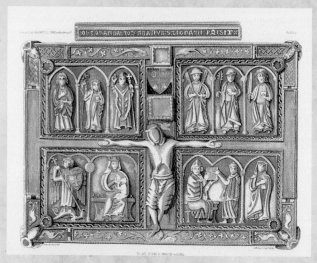

The *Domhnach Airgid* – a small section of gospel script dating back to near the time of St Patrick is the oldest example of Irish Latin writing now extant. It is named after its beautiful shrine ('the Silver Church').

THE LEGEND OF ST COLUMCILLE AND THE CATHACH

DESPITE A GREAT DEAL of investigation and discussion, there is as yet no exact date that can be attributed to the *Cathach*. The best that can be said is that it is a product of the early Columban monastic era. Most probably it goes back to AD600, but it could reach as far back as Columcille's time, between AD521 and AD597, back to when, in the young Irish Church, there was a great hunger for the latest scriptural writing from abroad — similar to the present-day drive to acquire the latest software of the computer age.

It is out of that hunger for new biblical versions that the legend of the *Cathach* grows. St Columcille was of royal blood, a warrior who could have challenged for high kingship but who instead became a dynamic man of learning, dedicated to the spread of holy writ to the widest possible audience. Not content to have others provide him with books, he became a scribe himself. He is so described in Adamnan's *Life of Columcille*, which was written less than 100 years after his death by one of his kinsmen, Adamnan, who was his successor in the Abbacy of Iona.

Columcille's love of books is exemplified by many episodes during his life — his determination to read and write during every hour, his voyage to Tours for a copy of the Gospels, his hunger for the written scripture. But none is more poignant than Adamnan's portrayal of his continuing writing almost to the time of his death in AD597: 'He descended the hill, and having returned to the monastery, sat in his cell transcribing the Psalter.'[3]

Adamnan's Life of Columcille

A KINSMAN OF COLUMCILLE, but born some 30 years after that saint's death in AD624, Adamnan was eventually to succeed him as Abbot of Iona in AD679. Sometime between then and his death in AD705 he wrote his *Life of Columcille*. In what was the hagiographic style of the time, he attributes numerous and sometimes fantastic miracles to the saint. But at the same time he also gives a vivid and fact-filled insight into the course of Columcille's eventful life. It is on his work that most of our knowledge of Columcille is based. In his Introduction he states, 'I will tell with all candour what I have learned from consistent narrative of my predecessors and on written authorities anterior to my own times or are what I have myself heard from some faithful and learned seniors attesting fact, the truth of which they had themselves ascertained.'

The last words he wrote were of Psalm 34, v. 10: '*That is good.*' And at his passing his good friend Forgaill the bard wrote:

'Our seer lives no longer
Our soul's life is hidden
Our keeper of life is dead
He has died our lawful leader
He has gone, our witness of the word.'[4]

Now what has to be called the legend of Columcille and the *Cathach* comes not from St Adamnan's account but from another Life of the saint, written almost nine hundred years later by another kinsman, Magnus O'Donnell, who was lord of Tir Conaill from 1537 to 1555. Since the *Cathach* was at that very time being used as a talisman by the O'Donnells for their forays into north Connacht and east Ulster, it is not surprising that Magnus would make every effort to associate it as closely as possible with their own blood saint — the mighty Columcille.

According to Adamnan's Life of St Columcille, the saint was a dedicated scribe.

Stained glass image of Columcille by the artist Richard King.

According to Magnus O'Donnell's rather fabulous version of events, Columcille was visiting his former master, Abbot Finian of Moville, and discovered that he had brought back from Rome a superb copy of St Jerome's 'Gallican' version of the psalms. He asked for a loan and instead of just reading it he spent a number of days making a copy of it. When Finian found out that this had been done without his permission, he was very angry and demanded back both the book and its copy. Columcille adamantly refused to give up his now much-prized possession. In order to break the stalemate between these two former friends, they agreed to put the matter before the King of Tara, Dermot Mac Cerbaill, who, just like Columcille, was a great-grandson of Niall of the Nine Hostages. But any hopes the saint might have had of getting a favourable verdict from a man whom he considered his equal were very much dashed when Dermot ruled against him in the long-remembered decision 'to every cow its calf and to every book its copy'. However, that was not the end of the matter. Incensed by this rejection of his claim, Columcille challenged the king and declared 'This is an unjust decision and I will be avenged.'

From that moment a state of war existed between the O'Donnells and the High King. Summoning their allies from the northern Ui Neil of Ulster and from the kings of Connacht, the O'Donnells amassed a mighty army and headed south with Columcille's copy of the Psalter as their battle shield. King Dermot mustered his forces and moved northwest to meet them. They clashed in fierce conflict beside the legend-steeped Ben Bulben at Cul Dreimne in the year AD561. Terrible was the slaughter and when the battle was over Columcille was sickened to the depths of his soul by the sight of the dead and maimed on the field of conflict. In great spiritual pain he went to his soul friend St Laisran, who gave him the severe penance of going into missionary exile in order to baptise as many souls as the fallen of Cul Dreimne. As a further penance he was never to set foot on the soil of Ireland again.

The distinctive profile of Ben Bulben in County Sligo near which the battle of Cul Dreimne was said to have been fought in Columcille's time.

Magnus O'Donnell goes on to clearly identify the *Cathach* of his time with Columcille's copy of the psalms when in his Life of the saint he says:

> 'The Cathach, moreover, is the name of the book which caused the battle. It is the chief relic of Colum Cille of the territory of Cinel Connil Gulban. And it is enshrined in a silver gilt box which it is not lawful to open. And whenever it be carried three times, turning toward the right, around the army of the Cinel Conaill when they are going into battle the army usually comes back victorious.'[5]

This legendary account of the *Cathach*'s origin became the long-accepted folk tradition in the matter and strengthened the belief that Columcille himself wrote the *Cathach*.

WHAT WE KNOW ABOUT COLUMCILLE'S LIFE

COLUMCILLE IS THE bridge between the old Druidic ways and those of early Christian Ireland. While St Patrick is much revered, he is still the 'Roman missionary'. Columcille, on the other hand, is the native son, who devoted himself to a heroic quest of blending the ways of the Celts with the ways of Christ. He was the Christian Cúchulainn to whom any wonder or achievement could be attributed by his biographers.

Born into the royal line of Niall of the Nine Hostages, he could have laid claim to the High Kingship of Tara. Instead he opted to be priest, scribe, builder of monasteries and missionary. But at times during his 76-year lifetime he reverted to the code of warrior, king maker and bard. A complex man, therefore, who was described by Adamnan as 'angelic in appearance, elegant in address, holy in work, with talents of the highest order and consummate prudence'.[6]

The best source we have for his life, St Adamnan's book, was of course penned in the mode of seventh-century hagiography. With the purpose of increasing the saint's fame, it recounts a wide variety of prophecies, miracles and angelic visitations. But at the same time it gives us an outline of Columcille's life and activities which can be accepted as fact.

He was born at Gartan, Co. Donegal, in AD521. His father was Felim, grandson of Niall of the Nine Hostages, from whom the O'Neill dynasty of Tara takes its name. His mother Aethnia was also of royal blood, being a descendant of King Cathair Mór of Leinster. He was fostered to a priest of Pictish origin, Cruisthnechan, who called him Colum, or the dove of the Holy Spirit. Later, because of his devotion to the Church, his fellow students are said to have added the Irish word *Cille* to his name. So he is best known as Columcille, although a variation of his name is Columba — the white dove.

His early education was under St Finian of Moville and from there he went to be schooled in the ancient legends by Gemman, who is described as 'a Christian bard'. He then studied with the other St Finian at the great school of Clonard and when finished there was ordained priest. Along with St Comgal, who was later to found the great scripture-centred monastery of Bangor, he spent some time with St Mobhi at Glasnevin but had to leave there and return to his own people in Donegal in order to avoid the plague which was raging at that time.

George Petrie's drawing of what is called St. Columcille's house at Kells, Co. Meath.

On his return to the land of the northern O'Neill, aged just 24, he launched into the first phase of his career as a founder of monasteries. To this end he made good and prudent use of his royal connections. The land for his very first establishment at Derry in AD546 was a gift to him from his cousin Aedh Ainmire, who was later to become King of Tara. It was another royal cousin Aed, King of Tethba, who gave him the ground of Dair Magh for his famed establishment of Durrow some seven years later in AD553. With great initiative and energy, over a 15-year period, he created hundreds of churches and monasteries all across the O'Neill-controlled lands of the northern half of Ireland — Clonmore, Swords, Lambay, Skryne, Drumcliffe, Moone and many, many more, culminating in his master foundation on Tara's doorstep at Kells. He was thus eulogised by the sixth-century poet Dallan Forgail:

> 'Three hundred he measured without fault
> Of churches fair, 'tis true
> And three hundred splendid, lasting books
> Noble – bright he wrote.'[7]

Whether as a result of his battle with the King of Tara or not, the next phase of Columcille's life was in exile when he founded the great missionary centre at Iona on the west coast of Scotland. He was then aged 42 and for the following 34 years he laboured abroad until his death in AD597.

From his base at Iona he spread the influence of his Celtic brand of Christianity not only into Dalriada but also into Argyle, Strathclyde and east to the Valley of the Tay. His successors at Iona would later go south into Northumberland.

His legendary vow never to set foot on Irish soil was somehow circumvented when he came home in AD575 to work alongside Aedh Ainmire at the Convention of Druin Cett, where he defended the traditional rights of the bardic order (some say he attached Scottish soil to his sandals for the period of his stay). At this event he was again the bridge between the two cultures — Celtic and Christian — and his wisdom won the day. It was a bard from that meeting, Dallan Forgaill, who was to enshrine his legacy in a 23-stanza poem of praise, the 'Amra Coluimb Chille', which is found in the *Book of Leinster*.

> 'By his wisdom he made glosses clear
> He fixed the psalms
> He made known the books of law,
> Those books Cassian loved.'[8]

Iona, off the northwest coast of Scotland, as it is seen today and where St Columcille founded his monastery in the sixth-century.

HISTORY
OF THE CATHACH

— AD500s —

This beautiful little book of psalms is forever a monument to Columcille's memory. While there is no contemporary witness from the saint's own time to corroborate the claim of his authorship, neither can it be definitively proven that it is not the work of his hand. In fact, there are more reasons for than against that intriguing *possibility*. He was a devotee of the psalms. What remains of the book was written by one person. As the legend suggests, it does give every indication of having been written in haste, and experts are agreed that the materials and the writing could date back to Columcille's time.

However, the most that can be said with certainty is that the *Cathach* was the fruit of Columcille's inspiration and is a very early product of the Columban monastic community. As his fame grew during the years after his death, so too did the reverence accorded to this sacred object so closely related to him.

During the five centuries immediately after Columcille's time, we know nothing of the *Cathach's* history. It was most probably left in the care of a kinsman *coarb* at Kells. A coarb was the chosen lay of a local ecclesiastical clan which claimed hereditary succession from the saint founder of a monastic settlement. The *coarb* exercised authority similar to that of a local king and in temporal matters superior to that of an abbot at monasteric communities like Kells. It is in this unique monastic town in County Meath that it emerges out of legend and into history for the first time.

— 1090 —

At the command of Cathbarr O'Donnell, it was enshrined in a metal box at the monastery in Kells. This lovely shrine still survives at the National Museum of Ireland and an inscription on it tells of its origin: '*A prayer for Cathbarr Ua Domnaill, who had this shrine made. And for Sitric son of Mac Aeda, who made it and for Domnail Mac Robartaig the Coarb of Kells.*' Following on from this, in a twelfth-century saga about the death of King Muirchertach Mac Erc of Tara, contained in the *Great Book of Lecan*, reference is made to the *Cathach* as being in the hands of the O'Donnells and that it was one of the battle standards of the northern O'Neills.

—— 1250 ——

A poem contained in the *Book of Fenagh* places the *Cathach* at Drumhome near Ballyshannon, where keepers of the book, the Mac Robhartaigh family, had been given land by the O'Donnells in the townland of Ballymagrorty.

—— 1422 ——

Fiordealbhach an Fhiona, who was head of the O'Donnells from 1422 until 1439, had the *Cathach* shrine refurbished. He is the same chieftain who appointed the O'Clery family of Four Masters fame as historians to his people.

—— 1497 ——

At the battle of Bealach Buidhe near Boyle, the *Cathach* was captured by the MacDermots of Moylurg and its protector, the Mac Robhartaigh, was slain. Two years later the book was returned to the O'Donnells.

—— 1567 ——

We know that it was again used as a standard by the O'Donnells in their battle with the O'Neills at Fearsod Mor in 1567, and, proving how dangerous a job it was to be its protector, again the Mac Robhartaigh with it was slain.

—— 1690 ——

It was carried away from Donegal by Daniel O Donel when he went to fight on the side of King James II in the Battle of the Boyne. Afterwards he brought it with him to France. In 1709, while at the Jacobite Court in St Germain, he received a new coat of arms from Irish herald James Terry (the same man who was claiming ownership of the *Great Book of Lecan*). In 1723 O Donel had the *cumhdach* or shrine of the *Cathach* refurbished and inscribed with his new coat of arms.

—— 1735 ——

Daniel O Donel died in 1735, leaving a wife and a 14-year-old daughter. He left the *Cathach* in the safe-keeping of the Irish Benedictine monastery in Ypres, Belgium, with the stipulation that it could only be claimed by a chieftain of his people.

—— 1780 ——

In 1780 a Reverend Father Prendergast, of the Augustinian church in Cong, Co. Mayo, helped Sir Neal O'Donel make a claim on the book, which had come to the priest's attention when he was a student in Belgium some years earlier.

—— 1813 ——

After a delay of 33 years, the book was handed over to the O'Donels of Newport, Co. Mayo, in 1813. The rightful ownership had been attested to by Deputy Ulster King of Arms, Sir William Betham, and in that same year he got permission from the owner, Connell O'Donel, to open the *cumhdach* and inspect what was inside. It had been firmly believed that the ornamental box contained bones of Columcille, and it was also a superstition that great evil would occur to anyone who opened it. Without incident Betham first probed the container with a wire and confirmed his suspicion that it contained a book. Upon opening it he found 58 leaves of the *Cathach* much damaged by damp but still in a very legible condition. The opening was not without controversy, however, since a Dame Mary O'Donel made a legal complaint against Betham in 1814 for opening the box, but this appears to have gone no further.

—— 1843 ——

After 30 years in the possession of his family at Newport, Richard O'Donnell donated the precious *Cathach* to the Royal Irish Academy. Ireland's oldest book remains in their care on behalf of the people of Ireland.

The Hill of Tara, where Columcille's fateful confrontation with the high king is said to have taken place.

CONTENTS OF THE CATHACH

THE *CATHACH* IS A BOOK with personality — so unique and distinctive that any page from it is eminently recognisable, even more so than its famed sister volumes the *Book of Kells* or the *Book of Durrow.* Indeed it is easy to match it with the personality of its reputed author Columcille — a man of purpose, exact in his goals, with flair and inventiveness to match.

One can indeed imagine him closeted away in a cell, furiously wielding a quill in pursuit of his own copy of St Finian's much-coveted manuscript. But this enthusiastic scribe, be it Columcille or some other, was not in so much haste that he could not pause at the start of each sacred psalm to invent an appropriate capital letter for the opening word — an eccentric V encompassing a cross for *Venite*, a trademark M for *Miserere Mei* at the top of the 56th psalm; a flamboyant D for *Domine Deus*, which commences the 38th. And so it goes; even when letters had to be repeated, he found ways of giving them a different persona in the new context.

The method of introducing these opening words is also unique — the first letter is large and then each successive one diminishes in size until the last blends with the proportions of the regular text itself. One can even imagine the scribe singing a word like *Venite* as he wrote, beginning with a

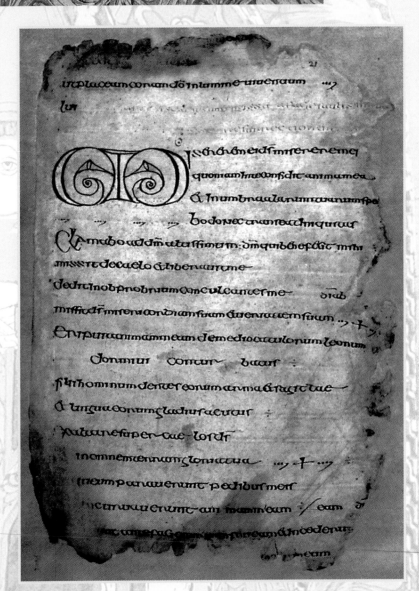

Psalm 56 in the *Cathach*, beginning with the words *Miserere Mei Deus* (God have mercy on me).

loud flourish that echoed around his cell and then gradually fading as the letters got smaller.

There are some extra colouring embellishments that appear to have been added later — red dots around the capital letters, rubric instructions at the head of each psalm referring to when it was to be used in choir and the spiritual meditation that should go with it. But these additions are mostly faded now and they neither enhance nor detract from the strong distinctive beauty of the basic text.

In its initial complete form we must assume that the *Cathach* included all 150 psalms, for in the ancient Irish Church, the monks had to recite the complete psalter every 24 hours. However, in its now curtailed state of just 58 leaves, the *Cathach* begins with psalm 31, verse 10, and, with a few interruptions and gaps, it ends at psalm 106, verse 13. Since we have other copies of this St Jerome Gallican version of the psalms, the missing psalms can be easily filled in.

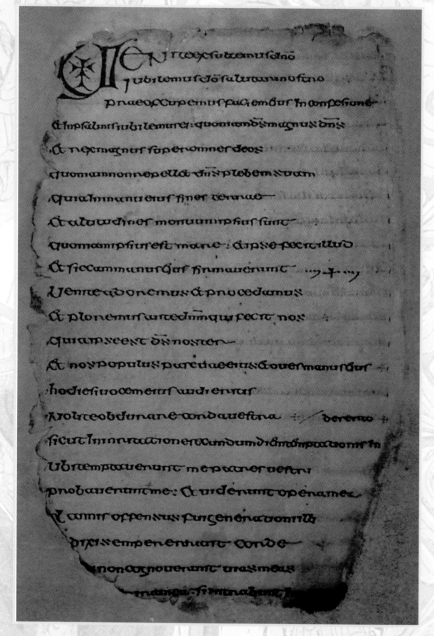

Another page from the *Cathach*, the *Venite Exultemus* – Come let us exult (Psalm 95).

But not the initials that went with them. One cannot even begin to imagine the beauty that is thus lost forever — what invention would our scribe have put into the B for *Beatus Vir* of the first psalm, for instance, or the L of *Laudate Domine* at the start of the 150th. We will never know, but in our unknowing we can only be very glad the inspiring beauty on more than 100 pages remains with us. It is no wonder that Columcille's kinsmen so loved and respected this book that it became their insignia, their intercessor, their protector and their 'Battler'.

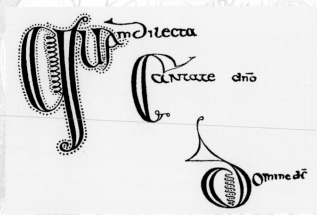

Was this simple art the work of Columcille's hand? We will never know.

CHAPTER VII

Divine Illuminations

THE BOOK *of* DURROW
(*c.* AD675)

and

THE BOOK *of* KELLS
(*c.* AD790)

WHAT WAS SOWN IN THE CATHACH FLOWERED INTO THE MOST BEAUTIFUL ILLUMINATIONS IN THE BOOK OF DURROW AND THE BOOK OF KELLS. FOR UPWARDS OF A THOUSAND YEARS, THEY TOO WERE ATTRIBUTED TO COLUMCILLE. BUT IN FACT WORK ON THEM DID NOT BEGIN FOR AT LEAST 100 YEARS AFTER HIS TIME.

Opposite: Carpet page from the *Book of Durrow*.

e do know that both of these works of art were created within the fold of Columcille's monastic empire, which in the seventh and eighth centuries stretched from Derry to Durrow and from the island foundations of Iona and Lindisfarne to Kells. The exact places of their writing has never been finally established but one thing is sure, the hands of Columcille's Irish monks are upon them and no amount of learned debate can erase that.

Both books are accorded the accolade of being the supreme example of scriptural illumination of their time — *Durrow* c. AD675 and *Kells* c. AD790. They are Gospel books and were created with the purpose of having the best and most beautiful copies possible for these four narratives of Christ's life. In the monastic chapels of Iona, Kells and Durrow, they were revered as living memorials of that life, second only to the Eucharistic presence in the Tabernacle. Their scribes displayed their own reverence for the subject at hand through a disciplined, robust, rounded and readable majescule (upper case) script. Their illuminators then added layer upon layer of intricate beauty, which elevated both volumes above the realm of mere book and into an Otherworld of pure art using techniques and influences from far beyond the Celtic Christian world in which they were created.

No doubt, both volumes were used for readings on certain very special days. In the case of *Kells* this must have been done by some specially trained lector who knew and understood the words that are so cleverly intertwined in illumination.

Reflecting the esteem in which they were held, both books had richly ornamented shrines created for them. Sadly, these have long since disappeared, but we do have contemporary descriptions of them that indicate lavish use of gold, silver and jewels in their make-up.

Both volumes represent a wonderfully unique fusion of the Celtic with the Christian, in which the free spirit of the Celt was still able to find full expression even within the confines of the established text of the four Gospels. Particularly in the case of *Kells*, the result is

Everything that had gone before was but a prelude to the exquisite perfection of illuminations in the *Book of Durrow* and the *Book of Kells*. We are here drawn into a Celtic/Christian art world in this opening page of St Mark's Gospel, which includes the lovely IN of *Initium* (Beginning) on folio 86 of *Durrow*.

an object that gives visual, earthy, artistic joy that is somehow detached from the sacred subject matter of the book. Attention might drift from the Gospel text itself, but one would never tire of feasting on the marvels of illumination.

THE BOOK OF DURROW

 HE *BOOK OF DURROW* has been described as the earliest of the great series of richly decorated Gospel books from these islands that have come down to us.[1] But at the other end of the spectrum, during its lifetime it was used by a local quack as a cure for cattle. Such again are the vicissitudes in the history of these great books.

This precious volume takes its name from the monastery that Columcille founded at Durrow in the latter half of the sixth century, some five miles north of our present Tullamore. Since it was his declared intention that each of his foundations

The Cross at Durrow in County Offaly, the sacred place where the *Book of Durrow* was preserved for generations.

Another reminder of times past at Durrow is this ancient well, named after Columcille.

should have a gospel book of major significance in its possession, it may well be that in fulfilment of that wish Durrow got its copy in or around the 100th anniversary of its founding, thus placing its creation sometime around AD680. Scholars vary a great deal in their judgement as to just where it was written. Some say Iona, others say Derry. But in actual fact there is no great evidence to suggest that it was written anywhere other than at Durrow itself.

Since no contemporary record of the book's writing exists, this is all guesswork.

HISTORY OF THE
BOOK OF DURROW

AD680

The creation of the Book is thought to be around this date.

AD877–916

The earliest time we can place it definitely at Durrow is during the reign of Flann Sinna, who was High King of Tara from AD877 until AD916. Just as his son Donnchadh was later to do for the *Book of Armagh*, he had a magnificent shrine made for the book and it is generally accepted that when he did this, it was then in Durrow.[2] This *cumhdach* has been lost since around 1689 but we do have a description of both it and its inscription, which was written into the book itself on folio 11v by Connacht historian Roderic O'Flaherty. A silver cross topped the shrine, and engraved on it were the words: '*The prayer and blessing of Colum Cille for Flann son of Maolsechnaill, king of Ireland, who had this shrine made.*'

1080–1547

Within the book itself there is definite evidence of it having been at Durrow in 1080 when a record of a land transaction by the monastery is written onto folio 248v. And there it appears to have remained until the sixteenth century. Like many other monasteries, Durrow was dissolved by Henry VIII in the latter part of his life, in 1547. But the book was kept safe somewhere in the general locality of the monastery.

1620s

In 1620, the O'Clerys wrote in their *Donegal Martyrology*: 'The Book of Columcille, called the Book of Durrow, a copy of the new testament in Irish letters, is at Durrow in the District of the MacGeoghegans with gems and silver on its cover.'[3] Sometime between 1621 and 1623 the Bishop of Meath and later Church of Ireland Archbishop of Armagh, James Ussher, used the book to collate its Gospel texts with those of the *Book of Kells*.

—— 1633 ——

Westmeath antiquarian Conal Mac Geoghegan of Lismoyne gave a vivid description of other, more urbane uses to which it was being put around this time. He saw the book at Christmas in 1633 when he wrote his name on the back of folio 124. Later, in his translation of the *Annals of Clonmacnoise*, he wrote: 'I have seen myself part of that book which is at Durrow in the Kings County in the custody of an ignorant man. When sickness came upon cattle, for their remedy put water on the book and suffered it to rest there a while and saw also cattle return thereby to their former or pristine state and the book to receive no loss.'[4]

—— 1646-1660 ——

In fact, the latter part of the book, from folio 208 to 221, shows signs of water damage, and a hole in the top right-hand corner of the leaves indicates that they could have been suspended by a thong in the 'cure' process.

Soon after this time the *Book of Durrow*, somewhat mysteriously, came into the possession of an associate of Archbishop Ussher's — a rather colourful individual named Henry Jones. At one time in his career he was scoutmaster to Cromwell in Ireland. He served as Vice-Chancellor at Trinity College from 1646 to 1660 and was appointed Church of Ireland Bishop of Meath in 1661. He is reputed to have been an excellent swordsman and was referred to as the 'Warrior Prelate'. Some eight years before taking up the Meath bishopric, during his term as Vice-Chancellor there, he presented the *Book of Durrow* to Trinity College.

—— 1677 ——

It was on January 10, 1677 that Roderic O'Flaherty made his notes on the reverse of folio 11 regarding the inscription on its shrine. At this time it was in Trinity but had no catalogue number and was referred to only as 'the Cupboard MSS'. Sometime during the next 20 years, and most probably during the occupation of Trinity by King James II's forces at the time of the Battle of the Boyne, the book was stripped of its valuable shrine, not the only thing that went missing at that time. In 1699, it was described by the Bishop of Dublin, Narcissus Marsh, as having been left in 'a plain brown rough leathern cover'. Why it was not stolen along with its shrine is hard to tell, but thankfully it was not and from that time until now it has remained as one of Ireland's literary treasures at Trinity College Library.

—— 1954 ——

In 1954 the book was carefully rebound at the British Museum in London by one of the world's greatest experts, Roger Powell. He cleaned and flattened the leaves, put them back in their proper order and removed a number of patches that had been placed over holes in the vellum. During the process he used 50 yards of linen thread and 50,000 stitches.[5] In 1960 Dr Luce and his associates published a facsimile and an accompanying commentary volume.

— HISTORY OF THE —
BOOK OF KELLS

— AD c.750s —

It appears certain that the *Book of Kells* was initiated at St Columcille's foundation on Iona in the latter part of the eighth century. At that time, this island, just off the coast of Mull in the Hebrides and some 80 miles from Ireland's mainland, was still in the possession of the Irish colony in Scotland.

This huge project demanded the calf skins from a herd of over 1,000 cattle and the involvement of perhaps five expert illuminators plus a large number of assistants. It could well have been planned as a memorial to Columcille on the 200th anniversary of his death in AD797. However, very soon after the work began it would have had to be interrupted as Iona sustained its first ferocious Viking attack. This forced the monks to flee home to Ireland for safety.[11]

— AD804-813 —

What had until then been only a small Columban foundation in Kells was rebuilt in AD804. Between AD806 and AD813 the Abbot of Iona, Cellach, took refuge there. We can only assume that the still unfinished manuscript was moved from Iona to Kells at this time. Some of those involved in its creation may well have perished during these years of upheaval, and some of the still unfinished pages of illumination may stand as memorials to them. *Book of Kells* expert Francoise Henry notes of this disastrous time in the book's history: 'It may also be that only part of the decoration was done at the time of the exodus, and that the fugitive monks continued their work in the new monastery.'[12]

In between raids on their traditional headquarters, the monks returned a number of times to Iona. So, along with other treasures, the *Book of Kells* may have crossed the Irish Sea many times. Following devastating raids in AD802 and AD806, the Columban community eventually abandoned the island. In AD806 Kells became their new Mother House and the home of this great book for the next 600 years.

— 1007 —

However, we can only guess at its movements during the first 200 years of its existence, since the first historical account of the *Book of Kells* actually being at Kells comes in the *Annals of Ulster* for the year 1007, and once again it was under threat: 'The Great Book of Colum Cille was wickedly stolen by night from the western sacristy in the great stone church of Cenannas [Kells]. It was the most precious object of the western world on account of the human ornamentation. This Gospel was recovered after two months and twenty nights, its gold having been taken off it and a sod over it.'[13] Some of the obvious damage to the pages may indeed date back to this unfortunate escapade.

—— 1140 ——

Confirmation of its being still at Kells during the later eleventh and the twelfth centuries was written onto blank spaces in the book itself in the form of Charters regarding grants of land to the monastery at Kells by Irish kings and local chieftains. One of these grants, dated around 1140, refers to a large parcel of land east of the town.

—— 1211 ——

As part of the reform movement that swept through the Irish Church in the mid-twelfth century, the monastery at Kells changed from Columban to Augustinian rule. In 1211 it was absorbed into the newly created Meath diocese, and became the parish church of Kells. And thus matters remained until the sixteenth century, when once again upheaval returned to Kells with the Protestant Reformation.

—— 1539-1568 ——

The monastery was suppressed by Henry VIII in 1539, and in the totally confusing religious situation which prevailed in Meath at this time it is very difficult to decipher what happened to the book immediately after that. The best guess is that the last Abbot of Kells, Richard Plunket, took the book under his care and that it was retained by his relatives during the next 50 to 100 years. Supporting this view is a note written on folio 334 in 1568 by someone identifying himself as Geralde Plunket. Whether he was of the same family as Richard Plunket we do not know. Neither do we know whether he was of the Roman or the Protestant Church.

—— 1586-1604 ——

During this period, the volume was used for the making of annalistic notes. On the blank page after St Luke's Gospel, a variety of hands entered references to events like the famine of 1586, the 12-year civil war during Queen Elizabeth's time, the accession of James I in 1602 and the plague of 1604. However, neither this material nor additional *intrusive* sentences written onto some of the main pages of the book by Geralde Plunket give us any hint of its adventures during these years.

An un-attributed note on the page after St Luke, dated 1588, gives the number of pages in the book at that time as '*two hundreds V score and iii leaves*'.

The Market Cross at Kells, which has been moved from its original precarious site at Market Square to a spot in front of the town's Heritage Centre.

CHAPTER VIII

Recalling the Ancient Tradition

BOOKS

of

THE BREHON LAWS

'THERE IS NO NATION OR PEOPLE UNDER THE SUN THAT DOTH LOVE EQUAL AND INDIFFERENT JUSTICE BETTER THAN THE IRISH; OR WILL REST BETTER SATISFIED WITH THE EXECUTION THEREOF ALTHOUGH IT BE AGAINST THEMSELVES, SO THAT THEY MAY HAVE THE PROTECTION AND BENEFIT OF THE LAW, WHEN UPON JUST CAUSE THEY DO DESIRE IT.'[1]

Opposite: A decorative page of Brehon Law text.

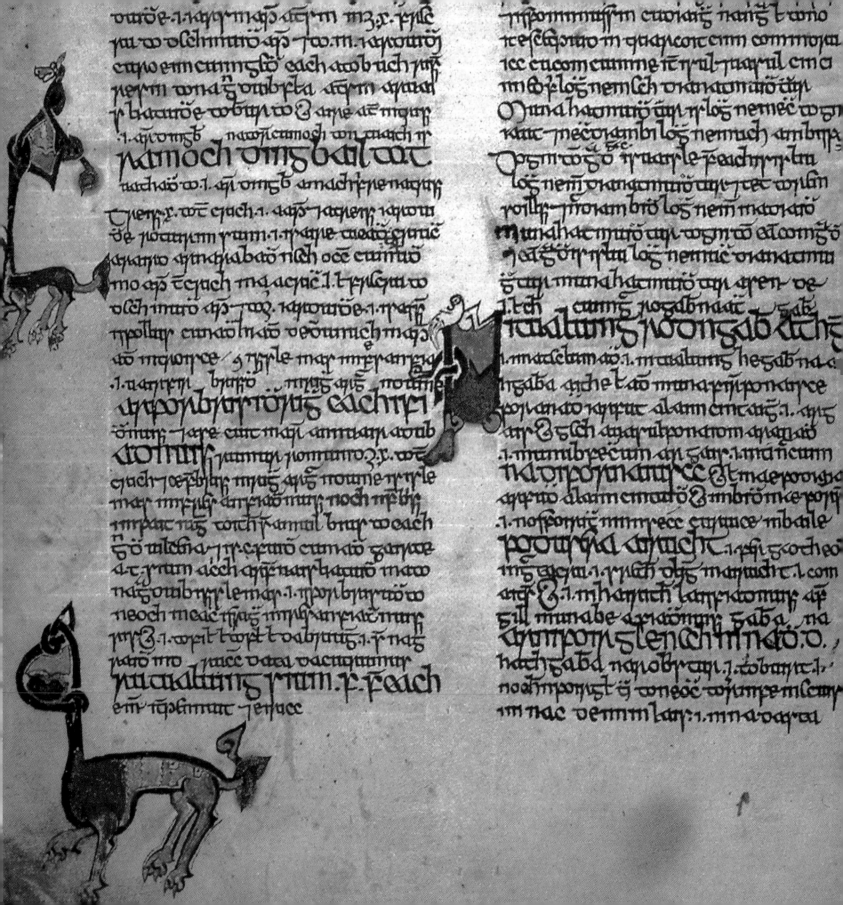

Ecclesiastics and the chieftains of Erin; for the law of nature had been quite right, except for its need to be in harmony with the Church and its obligations. And this is the Seanchus Mór. Nine persons were appointed to arrange this book: Patrick, Benen and Cairnech, three bishops; Laeghaire and Corc, and Daire, three kings; Rosa Mac Trechim, and Dubhthach, a doctor of the Berla Feini, and Fergus, a poet. Nofis, therefore, is the name of this book which they arranged, that is the knowledge of nine persons. This is the Cain Patraic; and no Brehon of the Gaedhil is able to abrogate any thing that is found in the Seanchus Mór. In it were established laws for king and vassal, queen and subject, chief and dependant, wealthy and poor. In the Seanchas Mór were promulgated the four laws: — the law of fosterage; the law relating to free tenants and the law relating to base tenants; the law of social relationship; also the binding of all by verbal contract, for the world would be in a state of confusion if verbal contracts were not binding.[5]

If it did indeed happen in this way, it has to be seen as a very shrewd move on St Patrick's part, for he brought together the most powerful kings in Ireland at the time — the King of Tara along with Corc from Munster and Daire from Ulster. There too were three of the most respected Brehons of the time plus Patrick himself and two of his most trusted followers.

While the Seanchus may not have been written down at that time, between AD439 and AD441 diplomatic meetings such as this could indeed have taken place and the memorised verses of the Brehon Law could have been adjusted over a period of time to coincide with the new Christian teachings. It may not have been committed to writing at that time but rather at a later date. It may not have achieved written form for perhaps 200 years after Patrick's era.

THE HISTORY OF THE SEANCHUS MÓR

The oldest known version of the *Seanchus Mór* brings us back to Christmas in the year 1350, when a very frightened young man named Hugh MacEgan was copying some of the commentary sections for his father Conor while a plague ravaged the country around Duniry, Co. Galway, where he was writing. We can in a very real sense join this young man in his scriptorium as he inserted this gloss at the bottom of page 36:

'One thousand three hundred ten and fifty years from the birth of Christ to this night and this is the second year since the coming of the plague to Ireland. I have written this in the twentieth year of my age. I am Hugh son of Conor MacEgan and whoever reads it let him offer a prayer for my soul. This is Christmas night. On this night I place myself under the protection of the King of Heaven and Earth, beseeching that he will bring me and my friends safe through this plague and restore us once more to joy and gladness. Hugh Aed Mac Concubair, McGilla na Naem, MicDuinnslene MicAodhagan who wrote this in the year of the great plague.'

there is still part to be made) amounts to over 5,000 close quarto pages. . . . This immense and hitherto unexplored mass of legal institutes regulated the political and social systems of a people, the most remarkable in Europe, from a period almost lost in the dark mazes of antiquity down to within two hundred years or seven generations of our own time (1861), and whose spirit and traditions influence the feelings and actions of the native Irish even to this day!'[7]

No original manuscripts of the laws like those of say the *Book of Armagh* or *Lebor na hUidre* still existed at the time when O'Curry and O'Donovan began their labours. The materials that they had to work with dated from the fourteenth to the sixteenth centuries and were copies of copies drawn from long-lost manuscripts that had been originally written around the seventh and eighth centuries.

The original language in which they were first written was called *Bearla Feini* (prior to the seventh century), and was very different from the Middle Irish in use when these laws were transcribed in monastery scriptoria during the seventh and eighth centuries. Later still, they were transcribed into more modern Irish during the fourteenth to sixteenth centuries in law schools like those of the MacEgans of Galway or the O'Breslins of Fermanagh. To further complicate matters, each law was accompanied by a great amount of commentary and glosses, which had been gradually added by learned Brehons down the centuries. Of these additions John O'Donovan himself wrote: 'I have to use a very powerful magnifying glass to read some of the glosses, which are written up and down, over and hither and carried into the margin in the most irregular and unsatisfactory manner.'[8]

Imagine all of this complicated material written on sometimes fading and crammed sheets of vellum coming before these two scholars O'Donovan and O'Curry. During the ten years of intense labour O'Donovan transcribed 2,491 pages of ancient text into his own writing and then translated it in 12 volumes. O'Curry was responsible for transcribing 2,906 pages, which he translated in 13 volumes. There could be no greater 'lovers' of Irish law than these two great men.

After their deaths the work was taken up by W. Neilson Hancock of Queen's University, Belfast, and Revd Thaddeus O'Mahony of University College, Dublin. Between 1865 and 1901 the resulting six volumes (over 3,000 pages in total), entitled *Ancient Laws and Institutes of Ireland*, were published. It is worth looking at each of these volumes just to get a flavour of the content of this ancient code.

Volume I (1865) dealt entirely with the Law of Distress, or the seizure of property for the satisfaction of a debt. In hundreds of individual sayings were laid down the manner through which our ancient Irish society dealt with the problems of vindicating rights and undoing wrongs, e.g. judgements were given about certain offences and then it was stipulated that there should be a number of days delay, or 'distress', prior to collecting restitution. There was this in relation to women: '*Distress of two days in the case of a daughter respecting the property of her mother, respecting the evil word of one woman against another, for securing the possession-taking by women, for there is no possession-taking by women but of sheep, and a kneading trough, and a sieve, for every woman from the other.*'[9]

Of households it has this to say: '*Distress of three days for using your horse, your boat, your basket, your cart, your chariot, for wear of your vessel, your vat, your great caldron; for 'dire' fine in respect of your house, for stripping your garden, for stealing your pigs, your sheep, for wearing down your hatchet, your wood axe; for consuming the things cast upon your beach by the sea, for injuring your meeting-hill, for digging your silver mine, for robbing your bee-hive.*'[10]

Volume II (1869) had the conclusion of the Law of Distress plus the Law on Hostage Sureties, Fosterage, the Law of Land Tenure, and the Law of Social Connections. In the latter the question was asked: '*How many kinds of social connections are there? Answer: eight. The chief with his tenants; the church with her tenants; the father with his daughter; a daughter with her brother; a son with his mother; a foster-son with his foster-mother; a tutor with his pupil; a man with a woman.*'[11]

Volume III (1873) included the final tract of the *Seanchus Mór — the Corus Bescna*. This is a part of what was called Customary Law or law that from time immemorial had grown out of the common customs of the people. This is followed by a long 500-page tract on ancient criminal law called the *Book of Aicill*. This is named after the ancient title for the Hill of Skryne near Tara in County Meath and in its introduction it is in large part attributed to none other than Cormac Mac Airt, who was legendary King of Tara from AD227 to AD266. Other judgements in the book are said to have come from Cennfaeladh, son of Olleil, whose time is some 400 years later in the mid-seventh century. He was wounded in the Battle of Moira in AD642, then wrote down these precepts at Toomregan in present-day County Cavan.

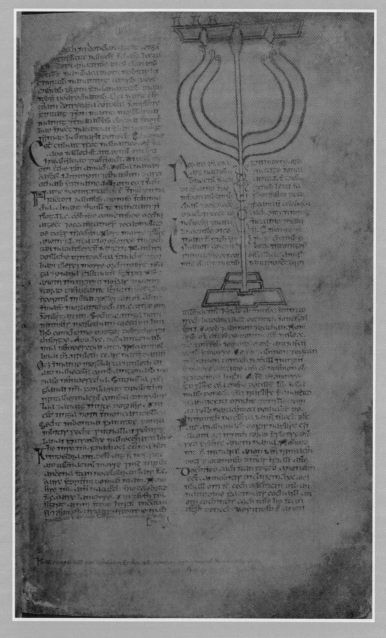

In addition to the Brehon Law texts, the learned MacEgan family of Duniry, Co. Galway, were also responsible for creating the *Lebor Breac*. This colourful page from it tells of the meeting of Moses with Niul, father of Goedhel Glas, who was the reputed progenitor of the Milesians. The image in the right column is of the candelabrum which illuminated the tabernacle of Moses and the Israelites.

In the *Annals of the Four Masters,* King Cormac is credited with having known the art of writing and it is said that he created a number of works: 'It was Cormac who composed works including the Teagasc na Riogh, to preserve manners, morals and government in the kingdom. He was an illustrious author in laws, synchronisms and history; for it is he who promulgated law, rule, and regulation for each science and for each covenant according to justice; so that it is his laws that restrained all who adhered to them to the present time.'[12] Recent studies have cast doubt on the previously accepted authorship of the *Book of Aicill.* Thus this story has to be taken as legend and read as such.

Images of what were termed the 'wild Irish' on the margins of John Speed's seventeenth-century map of Ireland.

Volume IV (1879) contains a selection of texts on family law, land law, the rights and obligations of members within a *tuatha* or clann. For example, in relation to fratricide, the normal laws of compensation for murder did not apply. If brother killed brother, the perpetrator of the crime would lose his 'honour price' and would in fact become worthless in relation to his kin. The house in which the crime was committed could be destroyed by his kin with impunity. In the laws of marriage there were 11 reasons for separation. For instance, if a man repudiated his wife for another woman, his wife was then free to leave him, but she also had the right to stay in the same house if she so wished. Also, a man could strike his wife to 'correct' her. But she had the right to divorce him if the blow left a blemish. Other tracts referred to bee law, rights to water, and land forfeiture for crimes committed. There was also a section known as the *Crith Gabhlach*, which gave detailed descriptions of the several social ranks and the organisation of the Irish tribes. Eugene O'Curry was of the opinion that this latter tract was first written down about the seventh century. It states that the number of classes of men is seven — two that are free but not noble and then five that are both free and noble, including various kinds of chiefs and then the king: '*A fer mhidbothman; a bo-aire chief; an aire-desa chief; an aire-ard chief; an aire tuise chief; an aire-forgaill chief and a king.*'[13]

Volume V (1901) is more general in its content under the heading 'Certain Other Selected Brehon Law Tracts', and these include what could be called 'teaching manuals' from the law schools. There is the 'Small Primer', which comments on judgements about *truth, law and nature* and again delineates the various classes of people in society and the honour price of the people in a household. This is followed by what are called 'The Heptides' — 100 wise sayings based on the magical number seven. For example, '*There are seven fathers who do not pay the liabilities of their sons, though it is from them they descend: a king, and a bishop, and a man from whom his sense has departed, a man who has departed from the world, and a man for whom his tribe answers, a 'fuidir' person* [semi-free man], *a poet, and a 'cu-glas* [meaning unknown]'.[14] Then there are tracts on Judgements, on Pledge Interests, another on the Confirmation of Right and Law and yet another entitled 'On the Removal of Covenants'.

Volume VI (1901) is completely taken up with a very important Glossary of Terms that runs to 800 pages.

CHAPTER IX

Immortalising Brian Boru

THE ANNALS
of
INISFALLEN
and
THE WAR *of*
THE GAEDHIL *with*
THE GAILL

'Superstar' of pre-norman irish history, brian boru's exploits are recorded in two major munster volumes written within the living memory of his grandchildren — ireland's oldest annals, the annals of inisfallen and the war of the gaedhil with the gaill (foreigners).

Opposite: Page from the *Book of Leinster* on the war of the Gaedhil with the Gaill.

'*Out of the book of Cuconnacht O'Daly the poor friar Michael O'Clery wrote the copy from which this was written in the convent of the Friars in Multyfarnham in the month of March of this year 1628; and this copy was written by the same friar in the convent of Dun-na-nGall in the month of November in this year 1635.*'[9]

From this it appears that O'Clery made two copies from the now-lost twelfth-century *Book of Cuconnacht O'Daly* and that the second of these is the one now in the library at Brussels.

In 1867, using all three available copies of the tract, James Henthorn Todd created what he called the 'Original Irish Text with Translation and Introduction of the *War of the Gaedhil and the Gaill*'. His work remains the definitive copy of this important document. It is divided into two main parts:

Chapters 1–40 — History of the arrival of the Vikings.
Chapters 41–121 — History of the Dal Cais sept and its most famous leader, Brian Boru.

The Tide at Clontarf: Proof of Eye-witness Account

JAMES HENTHORN TODD describes a unique experiment that he attempted in order to determine whether or not details given in the tract about the time of tides in Dublin Bay during the Battle of Clontarf coincided with what an eye-witness would have known. Without revealing the purpose of his query, Todd asked Trinity Professor of Geology Samuel Haughton to determine for him the hour of high water in Dublin Bay on April 23rd, 1014.

The detailed answer read before the Royal Irish Academy in May 1861 proved to the author's satisfaction that 'the truth of the narrative is most strikingly established'. He concluded from this that what was said in the book about the full tide coinciding with sunrise on the morning of the battle had to be an 'eye-witness' account, and thus the work of a contemporary author.

beside the Eske River in Donegal Town had been taken over by British ally Sir Niall Garbh O'Donnell and destroyed by a massive explosion in 1601, the Franciscans had fled to makeshift accommodation further south in the bay along the Drowes River near Bundoran. It was here, on the banks of the fish-rich Drowes, that Brother Michael O'Clery brought together his team of experts to begin work on what were then to be called the *Annals of the Kingdom of Ireland*.

Work started on January 22, 1632 and with the material then available to them, continued for one whole year. Either because of security reasons or the need to obtain the loan of more much-needed texts, there was a pause of over two and a half years until writing resumed in August of 1635. It is known that Brother Michael visited the Franciscan houses in both Ennis and Quin during the summer of 1634 to copy material from manuscripts like the *Red Book of Munster*.

We will never know all of the sources used by the Four Masters; some of them have since disappeared, while others have perhaps been renamed. However, we can with certainty pinpoint the following as having either been previously copied or physically present when the work was in progress: *Lebor na hUidre, Book of Leinster, Book of Lismore, Annals of Inisfallen, Annals of Tigernach, Great Book of Lecan, Yellow Book of Lecan, Annals of Ulster, Annals of Connacht, Book of Glendalough, Annals of Lecan, Annals of Loch Ce, Annals of Clonmacnoise, Cronicum Scotorum,* plus the following volumes which are now lost: *The Synchronisms of Flann Mainstreach, Annals of the Island of Saints, Annals of Maolconary, Book of the O'Duignans, Book of Cucogry O'Clery, Book of Maolin Og Mac Bruioclin, Book of Lugad O'Clery.*

For this list there is evidence either within the *Annals* or from notes in the volumes researched. In one of the introductory letters at the beginning of volume one there is a reference to 'other documents too numerous to mention'. These might include some volumes that were then in the possession of Archbishop Ussher, as well as others which at that time were still under the protection of Duald Mac Fir Bisigh, who loaned the Four Masters the *Annals of Lecan*. But he may have made many other ancient documents like those relating to the Brehon Laws available to them as well.

The Four Masters had to take refuge with the Franciscan community hiding out along the banks of the *Drowes River,* **where it flows from Lough Melvin toward Donegal Bay.**

IMPORTANT ANNALS
THAT PRECEDED THOSE OF
THE FOUR MASTERS

1. The *Annals of Tigernach* — these well-respected annals were begun by learned abbot of Clonmacnoise Tigernach hua Braein, who died in 1088. He collated the material from the Old Testament era of the Prophets Jonas and Isaiah down to his own time. Another scribe continued them after Tigernach until 1407. They are considered to be the most trustworthy of the ancient Irish annals. They were translated by Whitley Stokes in 1895–96.[10]

2. The *Annals of Inisfallen* cover from the time of Abraham down to the year 1319 and their writing began around the same time as the *Annals of Tigernach* (see Chapter 9).

3. The *Annals of Clonmacnoise* begin with the creation of the world and continue until 1408. The version of them available to the Four Masters ended with the year 1227. The only copy of them now existent is an English translation made by Connla Mac Echagan of Westmeath for Lord Delvin in 1627. They concentrate largely on the Invasion Legends and the exploits of Irish kings. There is no proof that they were written at Clonmacnoise, but that name was given to them by their translator Mac Echagan.

4. The *Annals of Ulster* were largely written on the Lough Erne island of Senait in County Fermanagh, but parts of them were transcribed in Counties Meath and Cavan. They begin at the earliest times and continue down to 1588. First written around 1489 at the behest of the Mac Manus family by hereditary historians of Fermanagh, they were continued in various hands down the years, including members of the O'Luinin family, in whose possession they were when used by the Four Masters. They are largely concerned with Ulster matters but they also give us some significant dates for events in other parts of the country like the arrival of St Patrick in AD432 and the robbing of the *Book of Kells* in AD1007. A four-volume edited translation of the *Annals of Ulster* was published between 1887 and 1901. The Dublin Institute for Advanced Studies produced the first volume of a new translation in 1983 covering the years up to 1130.

5. The *Annals of Loch Ce*, named for the great Lough Key in County Roscommon, were written on an island in the lake for the MacDermot family. Most of the text was composed around 1588 by members of the hereditary

Though stained with the blood of the patriot and martyr,
My blessing attend you!
My Blessing Attend you!' [13]

Following early education in one of the Gaelic schools that still survived, he, like thousands of young men in his time who wished to advance their learning, emigrated to the Continent. Some say he studied for a time in Salamanca but his later education was certainly at Bordeaux. He was ordained priest and gained a Doctorate in Divinity prior to returning home at about age 30 in 1610 to an Ireland in which religious intolerance wavered between threat and violent execution and back again under the ambivalent reigns of James I and Charles I. He took up his pastoral duties in his home county at Knockgraffon near Clogheen and later built a new church at Tubrid. His treatise on the Mass was written in 1615 and ten years later he completed a tract called the *Three Shafts of Death*.

He was a preacher of no mean talent and attracted large congregations. Among them on one occasion around 1629 was the lady lover of the despotic Lord President of Munster, George Carew. She took umbrage at the tone of his sermon and reported to Carew that it had been aimed at him. Carew immediately invoked a Proclamation against the priest, and Keating had no option but to go on the run. Under cover of darkness he was led away to hiding in the Glen of Aherlow by the rapparee Seamus Hogan. And there he remained until 1633 when Carew was recalled to England. It is during this four-year period of constant danger that Geoffrey performed the seemingly impossible task of writing his *History of Ireland*. He must have had the project in mind long before then and had long been collecting material from whatever of the ancient texts he could access. We know he had a fairly extensive library at his house, since it is recorded that when the soldiers raided it soon after his hasty departure with Hogan, 'they had scattered all his books about'. [14]

Somehow he was able to travel during those years in order to further consult the ancient documents. From the text itself we know that he read from the *Book of Leinster*, *Book of Cluain Eidhneach* (in Laois), *Book of Glendalough*, *Lebor na hUidre*, *The Yellow Book of Saint Moling*, *The Black Book of Saint Molga*, *The Red Book of Mac Aegan*, *The Speckled Book of Mac Aegan (Lebor Breac)*, *The Salter of Cashel*, *The Salter na Rann* and a book he calls the

Sample of Geoffrey Keating's handwriting

Book of Armagh, which may be different from the volume we now refer to by that name. A number of these texts are no longer in existence, hence the additional value of his compilation. We know that he travelled to Cork, Donegal and other parts of the north in his search for material. And no doubt he consulted many more books than are on this list.[15]

Keating's *History of Ireland* begins with the earliest times and covers down to the year 1170 after the arrival of his own Norman ancestors. In the construction of his work he uses mythology, fable, hagiography, genealogy, folklore and topography along with historical tracts. In some writings of the eighteenth and nineteenth centuries he was bitterly castigated for the manner in which he wove together these various strands of Irish lore in the creation of his fascinating narrative. For example, Mr and Mrs S.C. Hall, in their well-thought-of 1840 publication *Ireland, Its Scenery and Character*, disparagingly refer to Keating's *History* as 'a very silly heap of ill-digested fictions'.[16] In 1885 Charles MacCarthy Collins MRIA commented: 'In the *History of Ireland* each page is full of absurd traditions, impossible legends, preposterous chronologies, ridiculous genealogies, ludicrous miracles, extraordinary wars, "An extravagantly mad perform-ance", it has been called.'[17]

Yet writing less than 20 years later, David Comyn, in a preface to his translation of *Foras Feasa*, had nothing but praise for Keating's efforts: 'Geoffrey Keating stands alone among Gaelic writers; he has had neither precursor nor, in his own domain, either equal or second, His works show the fullest development of the language and his historical treatise marks an epoch in our literature, a complete departure from the conventional usage of the annalists.'[18]

TURBRID CHURCHYARD—BURIAL PLACE OF THE HISTORIAN KEATING.

INSCRIPTION IN HONOUR OF KEATING.

The little church at Tubrid, Co. Tipperary, where Geoffrey Keating is buried. The plaque above the door commemorates Geoffrey Keating and his fellow priest Eugene Duhy. It could serve as a memorial to all the unknown scribes who laboured down the centuries to preserve the ancient literature of Ireland.

'Pray for the souls of Father Eugene Duhy, vicar of Tubrid, and G. Keating, D.D., founders of this chapel, and also for all others, priests and laymen, whose bodies lie interred in this chapel, A.D. 1644.'

CONTENTS OF KEATING'S HISTORY OF IRELAND

GEOFFREY KEATING DIED around 1650 and is buried in the little church he built at Tubrid. Just as with Brother Michael O'Clery, the exact spot is not known. His handwritten original of the *History of Ireland* is now believed lost, but a number of excellent copies made by both himself and his friend Sean O'Maolconary of County Clare have survived. Using these, David Comyn and Revd Patrick S. Dinneen, between 1900 and 1913, produced a brilliant four-volume edition in Irish and English for the Irish Texts Society series.

Volume one, edited by Comyn, is a most lucid and flowing version of the *Lebor Gabála Érenn* and brings us from the earliest legends about Ireland down to the arrival of the Milesians or the Gael. He begins:

> 'Here I proceed to write of the history of Ireland and of every name that was given to it, and every division that was made of it, and of every invasion that was made of it, and every people who took it, and of every famous deed which was done in it during the time of each high king who was over it at any time from the beginning to this time, as many of them as I have found to publish.'[19]

If that would not encourage any Irish person to read on, nothing would. Volume two, edited by Dinneen, brings the story to the time of Niall of the Nine Hostages and his immediate descendants in the Kingship of Tara. St Patrick enters at the beginning of volume three, which ends in Norman times with the death of King John in 1216. Volume four is taken up with a genealogical tract on 'The Branching of the Sons of Milidh', a synchronisation of world history with that of Ireland, and finally a most useful index of the whole work, compiled by Patrick Dinneen.

In the face of what he termed 'lies' about the Irish written by the 'new English' like Cambrensus, Spenser, Stanihurst, Barckley, Davies and Campion, Keating set about giving Ireland a history it could be proud of. He invented nothing but neither did he leave any of the ancient traditions out. He did indeed apply some of the critical methods of Renaissance Europe to his task but this did not deter him. For he included what he knew was popular and for which there was no source or contemporary record other

than the origin legends of the people as preserved down the generations, first through oral transmission and then in the ancient books that he had consulted.

In his own lively introduction to the work, he compared people like Spenser and Davies, who
repeated falsehoods about Ireland and the Irish, to beetles who preferred wallowing in the dung of
untruth rather than seeking the delicate flowers of Ireland's story to be found in the primary sources.
This was a man fighting for a nation's soul, and time has proven that he won the battle. With all its
faults, his story of who we are and where we came from has, since his time, been the one we are most
proud of and most able to identify with. More critical histories there have been since his time, but when

you come right down to it, for the ordinary
citizen of Ireland, Keating's version is still as
good as it gets. In this we are no different from
the Romans with their tales of Romulus and
Remus or the Greeks with their Herodotus. His
reason for writing is set forth in this telling
sentence from his introduction: *I deemed it was not
fitting that a country so honourable as Ireland, and the
races so noble as those that have inhabited it, should go
into oblivion without mention or narration being left of
them.'*

In accomplishing that task he has done well.
In the centuries that followed, the spirit that
imbues his work has in large part to be given
credit for the resurrection from oblivion of the
nation he wrote about when it was at its point
of greatest danger of being obliterated forever
from the face of the earth.

All that I tried to write about in this book
comes to life in Keating, for his work is the
distillation and embodiment of what the ancient
books of Ireland contain.

And that is it!

FOOTNOTES

CHAPTER 1

1 Magnus Maclean, *The Literature of the Celts* (Blackie and Sons, London 1902), p. 108.

2 David Greene, *Great Books of Ireland* (Thomas Davis Lectures, Clonmore and Reynolds, Dublin 1967), p. 69.

3 Eleanor Hull, *A History of Ireland and Her People* (The Phoenix Publishing Company, Dublin no date), vol. I, p. 59. Note: In keeping with the above authors — Maclean, Greene and Hull — I use the word Lebor rather than the more modern *Leabhar* to denote 'Book' in relation to *Lebor na hUidre*, *Lebor Gabala Erenn*, etc.

4 Lady Augusta Gregory, *Cúchulain of Muirthemne* (Colin Smyth, Buckinghamshire 1993), Preface, p. 11.

5 John D.D. Healy, *Ireland's Ancient Schools and Scholars* (Gill and Son, Dublin 1896), p. 280.

6 R.I. Best, 'Notes of the Script of *Lebor na Huidre*', *Eriu* VI, 161 ff., 1912.

7 *Drom Sneachta* on p. 99 of the text and the *Book of Slane* on page 43.

8 Robin Flower, *The Irish Tradition* (The Lilliput Press, Dublin 1994), p. 100.

9 R.A.S. Macalister, *Cluain Maccu Nois* (Catholic Truth Society, Dublin no date), p. 48.

10 Eugene O'Curry, *Lectures on the Manuscript Materials of Ancient Irish History* (James Duffy, Dublin 1861), p. 186.

11 A list of these publications up to 1939 is included in the introduction to Bergin and Best's third edition of *Lebor na hUidre*, *Book of the Dun Cow* (School of Celtic Studies, Dublin 1992, 3rd. ed.), pp. xxvii–xxxviii.

12 Eeanor Hull, *Cúchulain, The Hound of Ulster* (George G. Harrap, London 1911), p. 10.

13 The term *soul friend* or in Irish *anam cara* used here denotes a deep spiritual friendship between two people which bound their very souls together and allowed them to share their deepest thoughts and emotions. In the Celtic Christian Church, the concept was used in relation to the bond between penitent and a spiritual confessor.

14 W.B. Yeats, *Collected Poems* (Vintage, London 1992), p. 16.

15 *The Four Masters*, *Annals of the Kingdom of Ireland*, translated by John O'Donovan (Edmund De Burca, Dublin 1998, 3rd ed.,) vol. IV, p. 1069. These massive *Annals* tracing Ireland's story from the earliest times until the year 1616 were written in Donegal during the 1630s by four master historians, led by Franciscan Brother Michael O'Clery. They will be fully treated in Chapter 10.

16 Ibid., *The Four Masters*, vol. II, p. 983.

17 The Franciscan John Colgan wrote the lives of Irish saints, his *Acta Sanctorum*, at Louvain in 1645, based largely on material that Brother Michael O'Clery had sent over from Ireland during the previous 16 years. Geoffrey Keating, whose great work will be outlined in Chapter 10, was an innovative Irish historian who laboured contemporaneously with the Four Masters in the seventeenth century. His *History of Ireland*, called *Foras feasa ar Éirinn*, is a classic to this day.

18 George Petrie, *History and Antiquities of Tara Hill* (Hodges and Smith, Dublin 1839), p. 45.

19 *Lebor na hUidre*, *Book of the Dun Cow*, edited by Osborn Bergin and R.I. Best (Royal Irish Academy, Dublin 1929).

CHAPTER 2

1 Op. cit., Petrie, *History and Antiquities of Tara Hill*, p. 196.

2 Op. cit., O'Curry, *Manuscript Materials of Ancient Irish History*, p. 186.

3 Ibid., p. 188.

4 William O'Sullivan, 'Notes On the Scripts and Make-up of the *Book of Leinster*', *Celtica* VII (1966), pp. 1–31.

5 Op. cit., O'Curry, *Manuscript Materials of Ancient Irish History*, p. 584.

6 John Healy, *Ireland's Ancient Schools and Scholars* (Sealy, Bryers & Walker, Dublin, 1896), p. 515.

7 Charles Dunn, 'Ireland and the Twelfth-Century Renaissance', *University of Toronto Quarterly*, vol. XXIV, no. 1 (1954), translation p. 71.

8 Myles Dillon, *The Cycle of Kings* (Oxford University Press 1946), p. 25.

9 Edward Gwynn, *The Metrical Dindshenchas* (Todd Lecture Series, Royal Irish Academy, Dublin 1903), Part 1, Tara Poem IV (translation from *Book of Leinster*), p. 37.

10 Daragh Smyth, *A Guide to Irish Mythology* (Irish Academic Press, Dublin 1988), p. 124.

11 W.B. Yeats, *Collected Poems* (Vintage Classics, London 1989), p. 371.

12 Op. cit., Gwynn, *The Metrical Dindshenchas* (translation from *Book of Leinster*), p. 31.

CHAPTER 3

1 Op. cit., O'Curry, *Manuscript Materials of Ancient Irish History*, p. 189.

2 Ibid., p. 190.

3 Dermot MacDermot, *Mac Dermot of Moylurg: The Story of a Connaught Family* (Drumlin Publications 1990), p. 399.

4 Eleanor Hull (trans.), *A Text Book of Irish Literature* (M.H. Gill, Dublin, n.d. — c. 1910), p. 247.

5 Timothy O'Neill, *The Irish Hand* (The Dolmen Press, Portlaoise 1984), p. 38.

6 Op. cit., O'Curry, *Manuscript Materials of Ancient Irish History*, p. 189.

7 Douglas Hyde, *A Literary History of Ireland* (T. Fisher Unwin, London 1899), p. 249.

8 R.A. Breathnach, 'The Book of Ui Mhaine', in *Great Books of Ireland* (Mercier Press, Cork 1967), p. 77.

9 Op. cit., Hyde, *A Literary History of Ireland*, p. 249.

10 The Marquis MacSwiney, 'Notes on the History of the Book of Lecan', *Proceedings of the Royal Irish Academy*, vol. XXXVIII, section C (April 1928), p. 32.

11 Ibid.

12 Ibid., p. 37.

13 Desmond Clarke, 'The Library', in *The Royal Dublin Society, 1731–1981*, edited by James Meenan and Desmond Clark (Gill and Macmillan, 1981), p. 76.

14 Op. cit., O'Curry, *Manuscript Materials of Ancient Irish History*, p. 162.

CHAPTER 4

1 Thomas McLaughlan, *The Dean of Lismore's Book* (Edmonston and Douglas, Edinburgh 1862), p. 1.
2 Op. cit., Maclean, *The Literature of the Celts*, p. 185.
3 James Macpherson, *The Works of Ossian the Son of Fingal* (T. Becket and P.A. Derondt, London 1765, 3rd ed.), p. 253.
4 Aodh de Blacam, *Gaelic Literature Surveyed* (Talbot Press, Dublin 1929), p. 79.
5 Ann Dooley and Harry Roe (eds), *Tales of the Ancients of Ireland (Acallam na Senórach)* (Oxford Press, 1999).
6 Whitley Stokes, *Lives of the Saints from the Book of Lismore* (Clarendon Press, Oxford 1890), p. 149.
7 Op. cit., O'Curry, *Manuscript Materials of Ancient Irish History*, p. 197.
8 Ibid., p. 198.
9 Op. cit., Stokes, *Lives of the Saints*, p. 162.
10 Ibid., p. 183.
11 Ibid., p. 268.

CHAPTER 5

1 Ludwig Bieler, 'The Book of Armagh', in *Great Books of Ireland* (Clonmore and Reynolds, Dublin 1967), p. 59.
2 *Liber Ardmachanus, The Book of Armagh*, edited by John Gwynn (Royal Irish Academy, Dublin, 1913), introduction p. ciii. Note that the use of the term Scotia to denote the Irish of both Ireland and Scotland was common from a very early time and was still the norm at the time of Brian Boru's visit to Armagh. Its derivation is unclear but some historians feel that it could be a corruption of Scythia, which in the Milesian legends was the place of origin of the Gael.
3 Alice Curtayne, *The Trial of Oliver Plunkett* (Sheed and Ward, New York 1953), p. 56.
4 J.T. Gilbert, *National Manuscripts of Ireland* (Ordnance Office, Southampton 1874), p. cx.
5 Op. cit., *Liber Ardmachanus*, p. cx.
6 Ibid., p. lxxvi.
7 Newport J.D. White, *The Latin Writings of St Patrick* (University Press, Dublin 1905), p. 260 ff.
8 William Bullen Morris, *Ireland and St Patrick* (Burns and Oates Ltd, London 1891).

CHAPTER 6

1 A. Gwynn, *Celt and Roman* (The Educational Company of Ireland, Dublin 1922), p. 2.
2 R.A.S. Macalister, *Corpus Inscriptionum Insularum Celticarum* (Four Courts Press, Dublin 1995). Also George M. Atkinson (ed.), *Ogam Inscribed Monuments of the Gaedhil* (George Bell, London 1879), Introduction.
3 *Life of Columba by Adamnan*, edited by Daniel MacCarthy (James Duffy, Dublin 1861), p. 174.
4 *New Oxford Book of Irish Verse*, edited by Thomas Kinsella (Oxford University Press, Oxford 1989), p. 5.
5 Michael Herity and Aidan Breen, *The Cathach of Colum Cille, An Introduction* (Royal Irish Academy, Dublin 2002), p. 3.

6 Op. cit., *Life of Columba by Adamnan*, p. 5.
7 Translation of poem from *Lebor na hUidre*, in Ian Finlay, *Columba* (Victor Gallancz, London 1979), p. 75.
8 Op. cit., Herity/Breen, *The Cathach of Colum Cille*, p. 4; and *New Oxford Book of Irish Verse*, p. 4.

CHAPTER 7

1 William O'Sullivan, 'The Book of Kells', in *Great Books of Ireland* (Clonmore and Reynolds, Dublin 1967), p. 4.
2 Bernard Meehan, *The Book of Durrow* (Town House, Dublin 2000), p. 13; and op. cit. O'Sullivan, 'The Book of Kells', p. 5.
3 Op. cit., Gilbert, *National Manuscripts*, p. viii.
4 Ibid.
5 Op. cit., Meehan, *The Book of Durrow*, p. 76.
6 Op. cit., Gilbert, *National Manuscripts*, p. ix.
7 Francoise Henry, *Irish Art in the Early Christian Period* (Methuen, London 1940), p. 148.
8 Bruce Arnold, *A Concise History of Irish Art* (Thames and Hudson, London 1969), p. 38.
9 Peter Brown, *The Book of Kells* (Thames and Hudson, London 1980), p. 7.
10 Giraldus Cambrensis, *Topographia Hibernia*, 1185.
11 Magnus Magnusson, *Vikings* (E.P. Dutton, New York 1980), p. 32.
12 Op. cit., Henry, *Irish Art in the Early Christian Period*, p. 149.
13 *The Annals of Ulster to AD1131*, edited by Sean Mac Airt and Gearoid MacNiocaill (Dublin Institute for Advanced Studies 1983), p. 439.
14 Op. cit., Brown, *The Book of Kells*, p. 94.
15 Op. cit., Henry, *Irish Art in the Early Christian Period*, p. 154.

CHAPTER 8

1 Henry Morley (ed.), *Ireland Under Elizabeth and James the First* (George Routledge and Son, London 1890), p. 54.
2 Francis J. Byrne, *Irish Kings and High Kings* (Batsford Ltd, London 1987), p. 7.
3 T.G.E. Powell, *The Celts* (Thames and Hudson, London 1985), p. 185.
4 *Ancient Laws of Ireland, Seanchus Mór*, 6 vols (Alexander Thom, Dublin 1865–1901), vol. III, p. x.
5 Ibid., vol. I, pp. 2–17.
6 Op. cit., O'Neill, *The Irish Hand*, p. 32; and Kelly, Fergus, *A Guide to Early Irish Law* (Dublin Institute for Advanced Studies, Dublin 2003), p. 226.
7 Op. cit., O'Curry, *Manuscript Materials of Ancient Irish History*, p. 201.
8 Op. cit., *Ancient Laws of Ireland*, vol. I, p. xxxiii.
9 Ibid., vol. I, p. 147.
10 Ibid., p. 167.
11 Ibid., vol. III, p. 345.
12 Op. cit, *Annals of the Four Masters*, vol. I, p. 117, for Anno 266, the reputed year of King Cormac's death.
13 Op. cit., *Ancient Laws of Ireland*, vol. IV, p. 299.
14 Ibid., vol. V, p. 235.
15 Op. cit., O'Curry, *Manuscript Materials of Ancient Irish History*, p. 201.
16 Myles Dillon (ed.), *Early Irish Society* (Sign of the Three Candles, Dublin 1954), pp. 52–65.

MacSwiney, The Marquis (1928) 'Notes on the History of the *Book of Lecan*', *Proceedings of the Royal Irish Academy*, vol. XXXVIII, section C, pp. 31–50.

McDermot, Dermot (1990) *MacDermot of Moylurg: The Story of a Connaught Family*, Drumlin Publications.

McGarry, James (1965) *The Castle of Heroes of Loch Key*, Roscommon Herald.

McLaughlin, Mark G. (1980) *The Wild Geese: Irish Brigades of France and Spain*, London, Osprey Publications.

Minogue, John (1993) *The Christian Druids*, Sanas Press, Dublin.

Murphy, Gerard (1955) *Saga and Myth in Ancient Ireland*, Sign of the Three Candles, Dublin.

Murphy, Gerard (1971) *Ossianic Lore*, Mercier Press, Cork.

Nicholls, Kenneth (1972) *Gaelic and Gaelicised Ireland in the Middle Ages*, Gill & Macmillan, Dublin.

O Floinn, Raghnall (1994) *Irish Shrines and Reliquaries of the Middle Ages*, Country House, Dublin.

O'Grady, Standish (1892) *Silva Gadelica: A Collection of Tales in Irish*, vols I and II, Williams and Norgate, London.

Otway-Ruthven, A. J. (1968) *A History of Medieval Ireland*, Ernest Benn Ltd, London.

Richter, Michael (1988) *Medieval Ireland: The Enduring Tradition*, Macmillan, London.

Ua Ceallaigh, Sean (ed.) (1911) *Leabharna Loitheadh: A Collection of Ossianic Poems*, Gill, Dublin.

Wallace, Pat and Ó Floinn, Raghnall (eds) (2002) *Treasures of the National Museum of Ireland*, Gill & Macmillan, Dublin.

CHAPTER 4

Berleth, Richard (1978) *The Twilight of the Lords: An Irish Chronicle*, Barnes and Noble, New York.

De Vere, Aubrey (1905) *Legends of St Patrick*, Burns & Oates, London.

Dooley, Ann and Harry Roe (1999) *Tales of the Elders of Ireland*, Oxford University Press.

Macpherson, James (1765) *The Works of Ossian the Son of Fingal* (3rd ed.), T. Becket and P.A. Derondt, London.

McLaughlan, Thomas (1862) *The Dean of Lismore's Book*, Edmonston and Douglas, Edinburgh.

Murphy, Gerard (1959) 'Acallamh na Senórach', in *Irish Sagas*, ed. Myles Dillan, Stationery Office, Dublin.

O'Grady, Standish (1892) *Silva Gadelica: A Collection of Tales in Irish*, vols I and II, Williams and Norgate, London.

Purdon, Edward (1999) *The Story of the Irish Language*, Mercier Press, Cork.

Saul, George Branson (1970) *Traditional Irish Literature and Its Background*, Buchnell University Press, New Jersey.

Stokes, Whitley (1890) *Lives of the Saints from the Book of Lismore*, Clarendon Press, Oxford.

The Book of MacCarthaigh Riabhach otherwise The Book of Lismore, collotype facsimile, introduction by R.A.S. Macalister (1950) Stationery Office, Dublin.

The New Oxford Book of Irish Verse, edited by Thomas Kinsella (1989) Oxford University Press, Oxford.

Ua Ceallaigh, Sean (1911) *Leabharna na Laoitheadh: A Collection of Ossianic Poems*, Gill, Dublin.

CHAPTER 5

Ardill, John (1931) *St Patrick AD 180*, Hodges Figgis, Dublin.

Ardill, John (1932) *The Date of St Patrick*, Church of Ireland Publications, Dublin.

Bieler, Edward (1967) 'The Book of Armagh', in *Great Books of Ireland*, Clonmore and Reynolds, Dublin.

Bury, J.B. (1913) *A Life of St Patrick (Colgan's Tertia Vita)*, Transactions of the Royal Irish Academy, vol. 32, section C, part III, Dublin.

Chamberlain, G.A. (1932) *St Patrick: His Life and Work*, Association for the Promotion of Christian Knowledge, Dublin.

Concannon, Mrs. T. (1935) *Blessed Oliver Plunkett*, Browne and Nolan, Dublin.

Curtayne, Alice (1953) *The Trial of Oliver Plunkett*, Sheed and Ward, New York.

Davies, Dewi (n.d.) *Welsh Place-Names and Their Meanings*, The Cambrian News, Aberystwyth.

Fox, Cyril (1950) *Ancient Monuments of South Wales*, Stationery Office, London.

Hopkin, Alannah (1990) *The Living Legend of St Patrick*, Grafton Books, London.

Hyde, Douglas (1920) *The Story of Early Gaelic Literature*, T. Fisher Unwin, London.

Liber Ardmachanus, The Book of Armagh, edited by John Gwynn (1913), Royal Irish Academy, Dublin.

Luddy, Abbe J., (1930) *Life of St Malachy*, Gill and Son, Dublin.

Morris, William Bullen (1891) *Ireland and St Patrick*, Burns & Oates Ltd, London.

Ni Dhomhnaill, Cait (1975) *Duanaireacht*, Oifig an tSolathair, Dublin.

O'Grady, Standish (1892) *Silva Gadelica: A Collection of Tales in Irish*, vols I and II, Williams and Norgate, London.

Salmon, John (1897) *The Ancient Irish Church*, Gill and Son, Dublin.

Van de Weyer, Robert (1990) *Celtic Fire: An Anthology of Celtic Christian Literature*, Darton Longman Todd, London.

Walsh, Paul (ed.) (1932) *Saint Patrick AD 432–1932: A Fifteenth Centenary Memorial Book*, Catholic Truth Society, Dublin.

White, Newport J.D. (1905) *The Latin Writings of St Patrick*, University Press, Dublin.

CHAPTER 6

(1861) *Life of St Columba by Adamnan* (edited by Daniel MacCarthy), James Duffy, Dublin.

Ashe Fitzgerald, Mairead (1997) *The World of Columcille, also known as Columba*, The O'Brien Press, Dublin.

Atkinson, George M. (ed.) (1879) *Ogam Inscribed Monuments of the Gaedhil*, illustrations Richard Bolt Brash, George Bell, London.

Dillon, Myles, and Chadwick, Nora (2000) *The Celtic Realms*, Phoenix Press, London.

Dunlop, Eileen (1992) *Tales of St Columba*, Poolbeg, Dublin.

Ellis, Peter Berresford (1999) *Erin's Blood Royal: The Gaelic Noble Dynasties of Ireland*, Constable, London.

Farren, Robert (1944) *The First Exile*, Sheed & Ward, London

Finlay, Ian (1979) *Columba*, Victor Gallancz, London.

Gregory, John (1999) *The Life of Columba by Adamnan*, Wolfhound Press, Dublin.

Gwynn, A. (1922) *Celt and Roman*, The Educational Company of Ireland, Dublin.

Herity, Michael, and Breen, Aidan (2002) *The Cathach of Colum Cille, An Introduction*, Royal Irish Academy, Dublin.

Macalister, R.A.S. (1995) *Corpus Inscriptionum Insularum Celticarum*, Four Courts Press, Dublin.

Macnicol, Eona (1954) *Colum of Derry*, Sheed and Ward, London.

Simms, G.O. (1963) *Psalms In the Days of Saint Columba*, Association for the Promotion of Christian Knowledge, Dublin.

The Book of Common Prayer (1861) Oxford University Press, Oxford.

The New Oxford Book of Irish Verse (1986) edited by Thomas Kinsella, Oxford University Press, Oxford.

CHAPTER 7

Arnold, Bruce (1969) *A Concise History of Irish Art*, Thames and Hudson, London.

Battersby, William (1995) *The Book of Kells: A New Look*, Cannon Row, Navan.

Brown, Peter (1980) *The Book of Kells*, Thames and Hudson, London.

Byrne, Michael (ed.) (1994) *Durroe in History: A Celebration of What Went Before*, Esker Press, Tullamore.

Healy, John (1908) *History of the Diocese of Meath*, Association for Transforming Christian Knowledge, Dublin.

Henry, Francoise (1940) *Irish Art in the Early Christian Period*, Methuen, London.

Henry, Francoise (1964) *Irish High Crosses*, Three Candles, Dublin.

Liam de Paer (1967) 'The Book of Durroe', in *Great Books of Ireland*, Clonmore and Reynolds, Dublin.

McGrath, Fergal (1979) *Education in Ancient and Medieval Ireland*, Studies 'Special Publications', Dublin.

Meehan, Bernard (2000) *The Book of Durrow*, Town House, Dublin.

O'Fiaich, Tomas (1971) *Irish Cultural Influence in Europe*, Mercier Press, Cork.

O'Sullivan, William (1967) 'The Book of Kells', in *Great Books of Ireland*, Clonmore and Reynolds, Dublin.

Salmon, John (1897) *The Ancient Irish Church*, Gill and Son, Dublin.

Stokes, Margaret (1894) *Early Christian Art in Ireland*, Chapman and Hall, London.

Sweeney, James (1965) *Irish Illuminated Manuscripts*, Collins in Association with UNESCO.

The Book of Kells, With Study of Manuscript by Francoise Henry (1974) Thames and Hudson, London.

Walsh, John R., and Bradley, Thomas (1993) *A History of the Irish Church*, The Columba Press, Dublin.

Youngs, Susan (ed.) (1989) *The Work of Angels*, British Museum Publications, London.

CHAPTER 8

Ancient Laws of Ireland, Seanchus Mór (1865–1901), 6 vols, Alexander Thom, Dublin.

Byrne, Francis J. (1987) *Irish Kings and High Kings*, Batsford Ltd, London.

Carleton, William (n.d.) *Carleton's Stories of Irish Life*, The Talbot Press, Dublin.

Cusack, Mildred F., (1871) *The Life of St Patrick*, Longmans Green, London.

Dillon, Myles (ed.) (1954) *Early Irish Society*, Sign of the Three Candles, Dublin.

Dowling Daly, Mary (1997) *Traditional Irish Laws*, Appletree Press, Belfast.

Dowling, P.J. (1968) *The Hedge Schools of Ireland*, Mercier Press, Cork.

Herity, Michael, and Eogan, George (1957) *Ireland in Prehistory*, Routledge & Keegan Paul, London.

Hyde, Douglas, and O'Donoghue, D.J., (1918) *Catalogue of the Books and Manuscripts Comprising the Library of James T. Gilbert*, Brown and Nolan, Dublin.

Joyce, P.W. (1908) *The Story of Ancient Irish Civilisation*, Longmans Green, London.

Kelly, Fergus (1997) *Early Irish Farming*, Dublin Institute for Advanced Studies, Dublin.

Kelly, Fergus (2003) *A Guide to Early Irish Law*, Dublin Institute for Advanced Studies, Dublin.

Lodge, R. (1957) *The Close of the Middle Ages*, Rivingtons, London.

Mac Niocaill, Gearoid (1972) *Ireland Before the Vikings*, Gill & Macmillan, Dublin.

MacLysaght, Edward (1979) *Irish Life in the Seventeenth Century*, Irish Academic Press, Dublin.

Morley, Henry (ed.) (1890) *Ireland Under Elizabeth and James the First*, George Routledge and Son, London.

Wood-Martin, W.G. (1902) *Traces of the Elder Faiths of Ireland*, Longmans Green, London.

CHAPTER 9

Chatterton Newman, Roger (1986) *Brian Boru, King of Ireland*, Anvil Books, Dublin.

Cogadh Gaedhel re Gallaibh, The War of the Gaedhil with the Gaill, edited by James Henthorn Todd (1867), Longmans Green, Reader and Dyer, London.

Cruise O'Brien, Maire and Conor (1992) *Ireland: A Concise History*, BCA, London.

Gleeson, John (1927) *Cashel of the Kings*, James Duffy & Co. Ltd, Dublin.

Llywelyn, Morgan (1979) *Lion of Ireland: The Legend of Brian Boru*, The Bodley Head, London.

Llywelyn, Morgan (1997) *Pride of Lions*, Poolbeg, Dublin.

Mac-Geoghegan, Abbe (1849) *The History of Ireland, Ancient and Modern*, James Duffy, Dublin.

McGrath, Fergal (1979) *Education in Ancient and Medieval Ireland*, Studies 'Special Publication', Dublin.

O'Byrne, W. Lorcan (n.d.) *Kings and Vikings*, The Educational Company of Ireland, Dublin.

O'Muroile, Nollaig (2002) *The Celebrated Antiquary Dubhaltach Mac Fhirbhisigh, 1600–1671*, An Sagart, Maynooth.

The Annals of Inisfallen, edited by Sean Mac Airt (1988), Dublin Institute for Advanced Studies, Dublin.

Willis McCullough, David (2002) *Wars of the Irish Kings*, Three Rivers Press, New York.

CHAPTER 10

Annala Connacht, The Annals of Connacht (AD 1224–1544), edited by A. Martin Freeman (1941), Dublin Institute for Advanced Studies, Dublin.

Bergin, Osborn (1930) *Stories From Keating's History of Ireland*, Hodges Figgis & Co., Dublin.

Collins, Charles MacCarthy (1885) *Celtic Irish Songs and Song Writers*, James Cornish & Sons, Dublin.

Concannon, Margaret (1926) *The Historians of Ireland*, Irish Messenger Publications, Dublin.

Connellan, Owen (1845) *Annals of the Four Masters*, Dublin.

Cross, Tom, and Slover, Clarke (eds) (n.d.) *Ancient Irish Tales*, George G. Harrap & Co. London.

Cunningham, Bernadette, and Gillespie, Raymond (2003) *Stories From Gaelic Ireland: Micro-histories from the Sixteenth-century Irish Annals*, Four Courts Press, Dublin.

Dinneen, Revd Patrick (1902) *Irish Prose*, MacTernan Prize Essays – I, Gill & Son, Dublin.

Giblin, Bro. Cathaldus, OFM (1965) 'The Annals of the Four Masters', in *Great Books of Ireland*, Mercier Press, Cork.

Hone, Revd Richard B. (1834) *Lives of Eminent Christians*, vol. 1, *James Ussher, D.D.*, John W. Parker, London.

Keating, Geoffrey, *The History of Ireland*, edited by David Comyn and Revd Patrick Dinneen (1902), 4 vols., Irish Texts Society, London.

MacCurtain, Margaret (1972) *Tudor and Stuart Ireland*, Gill & Macmillan, Dublin.

MacLysaght, Edward (1979) *Irish Life in the Seventeenth Century*, Irish Academic Press, Dublin.

Meehan, C.F. (1882) *The Confederation of Kilkenny*, James Duffy and Sons, Dublin.

O'Brien, Fr. Sylvester, OFM (ed.) (1944) *Miscellany of Historical and Linguistic Studies in Honour of Brother Michael O Cleirigh, OFM, Chief of the Four Masters, 1643–1943*, Assisi Press, Dublin.

The Annals of Tigernach, translated by Whitley Stokes (1895/1896), 2 vols, *Revue Celtique* (reprinted 1993, Llanerch Publishers, Felinfach).

The Annals of Ulster (to AD 1131), edited by Sean Mac Airt and Gearoid Mac Niocaill (1983), Dublin Institute for Advanced Studies, Dublin.

The Four Masters, Annals of the Kingdom of Ireland, translated by John O'Donovan, 3rd edition (1990) De Burcas Rare Books, Dublin.

PICTURE CREDITS